Guide
Pub

Graham Cann

COUNTRYSIDE BOOKS
NEWBURY BERKSHIRE

First published 2018
© Graham Cann 2018

COUNTRYSIDE BOOKS
3 Catherine Road
Newbury, Berkshire

To view our complete range of books,
please visit us at
www.countrysidebooks.co.uk

ISBN 978 1 84674 362 7

Designed by KT Designs, St Helens
Produced through The Letterworks Ltd., Reading
Typeset by KT Designs, St Helens
Printed in Poland

Introduction

In this hectic, hurly-burly life, it seems that everyone is rushing around and barely able to engage with what is going on around them, as they dash from one place to another along busy, often jam-packed roads.

This book will take you off the beaten track and down a 'road less travelled', where the pace of life noticeably slows down. Here, you can take the time to explore Norfolk's windswept sandy beaches, meandering rivers, scenic heathlands, impressive clifftops, the stunning Norfolk Broads and so much more. Along with the striking scenery of the countryside, you'll discover, on or near the walks, Norfolk's rich tapestry of picturesque market towns and villages; its historic buildings such as ancient castles, priories and stately homes; and architectural feats like the Denver Sluice complex and some disused (as well as restored!) railways.

The Bull Inn, Little Walsingham

Guide to Norfolk Pub Walks

There are twenty circular walks in this book, each beginning and ending at a pub. In some instances, there was more than one pub in a particular location, but the one chosen, like all the inns, has been selected for its homeliness and character as well as for its good food and drink. The walks vary between just over two and just under six miles in length; because of the geography of the county, they are not too challenging, although, contrary to popular opinion, hills do exist!

My suggestion is that you take with you a good pair of boots, a backpack and some binoculars: there is a plethora of wildlife around the byways and bridleways of Norfolk, which is home to some of England's most acclaimed nature reserves. One of these is on the walk at the idyllic Cley next the Sea.

My sincere hope is that you enjoy each and every walk, and make many new discoveries in and about this wonderful county of Norfolk, which I have lived in and loved for nearly forty years.

Graham Cann

Publisher's Note

We hope that you obtain considerable enjoyment from this book: great care has been taken in its preparation. However, changes of landlord and actual pub closures are sadly not uncommon. Likewise, although at the time of publication all routes followed public rights of way or permitted paths, diversion orders can be made and permissions withdrawn.

We cannot, of course, be held responsible for such diversion orders or any inaccuracies in the text which result from these or any other changes to the routes, nor any damage which might result from walkers trespassing on private property. We are anxious, though, that all details covering the walks and the pubs are kept up to date, and would therefore welcome information from readers which would be relevant to future editions.

The simple sketch maps that accompany the walks in this book are based on notes made by the author whilst surveying the routes on the ground. They are designed to show you how to reach the start and to point out the main features of the overall circuit, and they contain a progression of numbers that relate to the paragraphs of the text.

However, for the benefit of a proper map, we do recommend that you purchase the relevant Ordnance Survey sheet covering your walk. Ordnance Survey maps are widely available, especially through booksellers and local newsagents.

The beach at Holme-next-the-Sea

1 Holme-next-the-Sea

3½ miles (5.6 km)

WALK HIGHLIGHTS

This sleepy coastal village is located on the North Norfolk coast, a designated Area of Outstanding Natural Beauty. The village is barely a few metres above sea level, and its houses feature two of the local stones: clunch, which is a hard form of white chalk, and carrstone, an attractive rust-coloured sandstone. These are often combined with cobbles, brick and flint to form a variety of patterns, which are seen on buildings throughout this part of Norfolk.

The beach at Holme-next-the-Sea attracted international attention in 1998 when a Bronze Age timber circle, which became known as Seahenge, was discovered here. Controversy ensued when it was decided to move the remains, some of which are now housed in the Lynn Museum in King's Lynn.

THE PUB

The White Horse, PE36 6LH

☎ 01485 525512 No website

Guide to Norfolk Pub Walks

HOW TO GET THERE AND PARKING: From the A149 Brancaster–Hunstanton coast road, turn off to Holme-next-the-Sea along Eastgate. Follow the road round into Kirkgate, and the White Horse is on your right. You can use the car park if the pub is not too busy – please enquire first. There is also parking along the road outside. **Sat nav** PE36 6LH.

MAP: OS Explorer 250 Norfolk Coast West. **Grid Ref:** TF 705433.

THE WALK

1 From the **White Horse**, turn right along the road, passing some attractive coastal cottages. At the T-junction, turn right, following the **Peddars Way** sign. Passing the linear village green on your left, cross the **River Hun** bridge; just after the bridge, turn left along a footpath beside a caravan park. Head straight on over a small bridge and then alongside a golf course to your right, with the river on your left. At the end of the footpath, turn right, and follow the tarmac road round to the left. Just before the golf clubhouse, turn right along a sandy path.

2 At a crossroads of paths before the chalets, turn right onto the **Norfolk Coast Path**. This magnificent route is rich in heritage, flora and fauna, pretty coastal villages and sandy beaches; it runs for 84 miles from Hunstanton to Hopton-on-Sea, south of Great Yarmouth. Follow the path for nearly a mile until you reach a walkway to your right, signposted **Norfolk Coast Path**. Take this path. Before you reach the golf course, turn left, again continuing along the Norfolk Coast Path. Look out for a small yellow arrow and acorn sign on the right along this path; turn right up the bank at this point. Follow the path round to the left onto the upper path.

3 About 200 metres past the last house, turn right down the slope into the Norfolk Wildlife Trust's **Holme Dunes** car park. Turn right and then left over a wooden bridge into **Redwell Marsh Reserve**. For the first 200 metres or so, keep to the hedge. Then keep to the drainage ditch on your right, and follow the path round to an iron gate, passing through a metal link stile. Follow this track to the road, and then proceed left back to the pub.

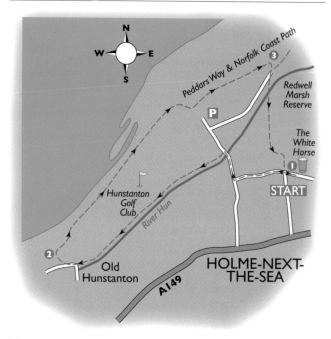

PLACES OF INTEREST NEARBY

At **Norfolk Lavender** in Heacham (www.norfolk-lavender.co.uk), your senses will be filled both by the spectacle and by the amazing fragrance of the fields of purple plants. All sorts of lavender products are on sale here; there are also animal gardens, a play park, tours and a tea room.

A little drive to the west will bring you to the town of **Hunstanton** (or 'Hunston', as it is known locally). There is literally something for everyone at this seaside town, from crazy golf to the peace of the Esplanade Gardens. It is well known for its uniquely striped cliffs showing different-coloured strata, for its magnificent sunsets and for being the only west-facing resort on the east coast!

The village pond in Great Massingham

2 Great Massingham

3½ miles (5.6 km)

WALK HIGHLIGHTS

Great Massingham is one of the most picturesque villages in the county, and is dominated by several large ponds, some of which have their origins as the fish ponds of an 11th-century Augustinian abbey.

After the outbreak of the Second World War, the RAF commandeered one of the biggest farms in the village in order to build an airfield. Blenheims were based here in the early days, and the airfield played a key role during the war. Today it is still used for private flying.

Like most churches, St Mary's has always been the focal point of village life, and not only for services: the porch was added in the 14th century and used as a schoolroom! Sir Robert Walpole, Britain's first Prime Minister, was educated here as a young lad. His descendants still live at nearby Houghton Hall.

The Dabbling Duck is a homely, welcoming inn; two of the owners are farmers, so you can expect locally sourced food and a good array of game dishes.

HOW TO GET THERE AND PARKING: From the B1145 Gayton–Litcham road, take the road to Great Massingham; the pub is on your left opposite the church. Parking spaces are available at the pub, but please ask first. Alternatively, there is ample parking around the green. **Sat nav** PE32 2HN.

MAP: OS Explorer 250 Norfolk Coast West. **Grid Ref:** TF 797229.

THE PUB
The Dabbling Duck, PE32 2HN
☎ 01485 520827 www.thedabblingduck.co.uk

THE WALK
Turn left from the **Dabbling Duck**, and after around 75 metres, just past the **Abbey Road** sign, turn left along a gravel-and-grass track. Eventually, it narrows into a smaller footpath; keep straight ahead. At a T-junction of paths, turn right. At the end of the path, turn left onto a concrete track leading towards the radio transmitters, and continue where it leads onto a gravel track.

At a T-junction of paths, turn right on to the **Peddars Way** path, which has fine views over gently rolling countryside. When you reach the lane, turn right, and keep heading straight on, past the 40 mph speed limit sign and some farm buildings on your left.

A hundred metres past **Hall Farm**, turn right along a footpath, and then follow it along a tree-lined path. After another 100 metres, take a footpath off to the left between two trees, running alongside a field. After the same distance again, cross the field towards a large hedge. Pass under the trees and across the next field towards some trees. Follow the path round, with a large paddock and house on your left. Just past the house the path veers right. Before the path crosses the field, turn left. Follow the path round towards some houses and onto a road. At the T-junction, turn right.

After 200 metres, turn left up **Mill Lane**; where the lane comes to an end, keep straight on until you reach the concrete runway. Proceed right, passing a large barn; 125 metres past this, turn right along a footpath

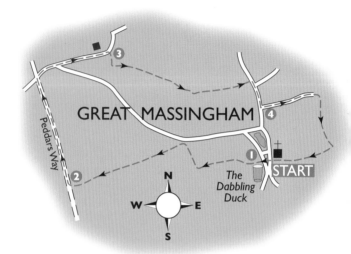

towards **St Mary's Church**. At the end of this path, turn left and then immediately right between some houses; you emerge on the road with the Dabbling Duck straight ahead of you.

PLACES OF INTEREST NEARBY

Two magnificent stately home estates are near Great Massingham. To the north-west is the royal residence **Sandringham** (www.sandringhamestate. co.uk), This country retreat has been a favourite of British monarchs since 1862. The house, museum and gardens are open for the public to enjoy. To the north is one of England's finest Palladian houses, **Houghton Hall** (www.houghtonhall.com), built in the 1720s for Sir Robert Walpole. The house, award-winning gardens and quirky sculptures keep this stately home one of Norfolk's most popular attractions.

Castle Acre Castle

3 Castle Acre

5½ miles (8.9 km)

WALK HIGHLIGHTS

Castle Acre is a quintessential English village with many charming cottages, a village green, a pub and a splendid church. It is considered one of the best examples of a Norman settlement in the country. Its name is derived from the walled castle built in the twelfth century: a stone country house was first built on the site, but soon it was decided that fortification was necessary, and so a heavily defended keep, stone walls and a large moat replaced the original building. The north Bailey Gate is still in existence. It is said that Oliver Cromwell's grandmother was a regular at the Ostrich, a 16th-century coaching inn with a wood burner roaring away to thaw out those winter ramblers.

THE PUB

The Ostrich Inn, PE32 2AE
☎ 01760 755398 www.ostrichcastleacre.com

HOW TO GET THERE AND PARKING: Castle Acre is off the A1065 north of Swaffham. Take the road to Castle Acre, driving under the arch of the Bailey Gate and turning left. The Ostrich is on your right. Please enquire before using the pub car park. **Sat nav** PE32 2AE.

MAP: OS Explorer 238 Dereham & Aylsham. **Grid Ref:** TF 816151.

THE WALK

1 From the **Ostrich**, turn right, and follow the **High Street** towards **St James's Church**. Turn left down **South Acre Road**, and follow it down to just before you reach the **River Nar** and the ford across it. Turn left across a footbridge, and follow the river path across scenic water meadows. The path will soon part company with the river and head towards a gate, which you pass through. Turn right onto **Blind Lane**, and then turn right along the road and over the river.

2 After 100 metres, rather than veering right, go straight on along the lane signposted to **Sporle** and **Little Dunham**. Climb the bank and walk along the field edge running parallel to the lane. Cross the A1065 onto another lane; once again, enter the field and walk parallel to the lane along the field edge. Your path soon begins to diverge from the lane, veering left with a copse on the right. Follow the path around the copse. Keep following the path with the hedge on your right.

3 When you reach the road, turn left towards **Newton**, and continue for just over three quarters of a mile. On the way, you'll glimpse a quarry on your right, where large amounts of chalk are extracted for agricultural and industrial purposes. Just before the A1065, turn right in front of a large farmhouse, and continue along the track up the hill. At the top of the hill, veer left. When this track peters out, turn left along the field edge, following a public footpath sign. At the bottom of the field, head for a gap in the hedge and then straight along a wooded path, eventually coming to **Grove Common**. Cross straight over the A1065, and walk down some steps and across a young plantation.

4 Once across the plantation, turn left at the T-junction of paths; your path leads to a driveway. Turn right at the T-junction, past the old site of **Newton Mill**, across the bridge and the tranquil area of the millpond, before veering left and following the lane across **Newton Common**. Some 350 metres up the hill, before the first house, turn left down a path signposted **Nar Valley Way**, a glorious long-distance path from King's Lynn to Gressenhall. Head straight down this path, ignoring any paths to the right and merging with a lane.

Continue to a T junction, and walk straight across onto a path and through a kissing gate; veer right, going diagonally across the

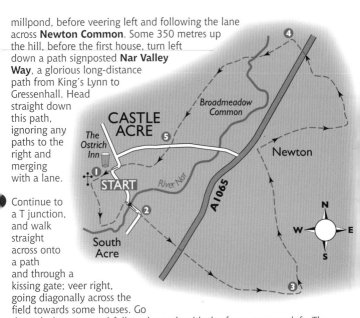

field towards some houses. Go through the gate, and follow the path with the fence on your left. The path will veer right and then left near the castle car park. The remains of this motte-and-bailey castle are well worth a look. Follow **Pye's Lane** up to the **High Street**, where you turn left to return to the pub.

PLACES OF INTEREST NEARBY

Castle Acre Priory (www.english-heritage.org.uk) is only a short walk to the west of the village. It is one of the best-preserved monastic ruins in England.

Shouldham Warren

4 Shouldham

4½ miles (7.2 km)

WALK HIGHLIGHTS

Shouldham is mentioned in the Domesday Book, and is situated in the lee of a chalk ridge that rises above the Fens in the west of the county. Evidence of an Iron Age settlement was found here in 1944. The 17th-century coaching inn, the King's Arms, is West Norfolk's first co-operative pub, and was voted Pub of the Year in 2016 and 2017 by West Norfolk CAMRA.

THE PUB

The King's Arms, PE33 0BY
☎ 01366 347410 www.kingsarmsshouldham.co.uk

HOW TO GET THERE AND PARKING: Turn off the A134 Lynn Road to Shouldham, following Mill Road and then Lynn Road into the village. The pub stands on your right, opposite the village green. The car park is available for those visiting the pub, but please inform the landlord. There are also parking spaces around the village green. **Sat nav** PE33 0BY.

MAP: OS Explorer 236 King's Lynn, Downham Market & Swaffham. **Grid Ref:** TF 676088.

THE WALK

From the **King's Arms**, turn left along the road. Take the first turning right into **Westgate Street**. A hundred metres past the **Post Office**, turn left along **Orchard Lane**, and go straight ahead into the driveway of the last house; then veer left beside a lawn towards a wooden gate. Follow the path for around 100 metres; then veer left, with a hedge on your left and a field on your right.

At the end of the field, go beyond the hedge, and turn right towards the conifer wood, following the track. At a T-junction of tracks, turn right; then, just before the track bends left, take a tree-lined footpath on the left towards **Shouldham Warren**, which is owned by the Stow Estate but managed by the Forestry Commission. Keep heading straight on. When you come to a deep ditch running to the left and right of your path, cross the ditch.

Proceed right along this path. When the path forks, take the left fork, away from the ditch. After 100 metres, you'll reach a T-junction of paths. Turn left here onto a wider path which circumnavigates Shouldham Warren, passing a colourful display of rhododendron bushes. Ignore any paths going to the left or right.

After a mile and a quarter, you'll come to a T-junction of paths. Turn right here. After a barrier to prevent cars entering Shouldham Warren, take the track on the right towards Shouldham Warren car park. At the T-junction, proceed left, heading towards **Shouldham** village. Keep heading along this road, and you'll pass playing fields on your right. Keep straight on at the road junction into **New Road**, which morphs

Guide to Norfolk Pub Walks

into **Eastgate Street**. Just past the village hall on your left is a medieval settlement including earthworks and buried remains. Two hundred metres further on, you'll come to the village green, where you turn right back to the pub.

PLACES OF INTEREST NEARBY

King's Lynn, the capital of West Norfolk, is a medieval port and market town with listed buildings, museums and cobbled streets housing merchants' homes. The tourist office is now accommodated in the prestigious Custom House, which dates back to 1683. King's Lynn was one of England's foremost ports, and sits on the River Great Ouse where it exits into the Wash.

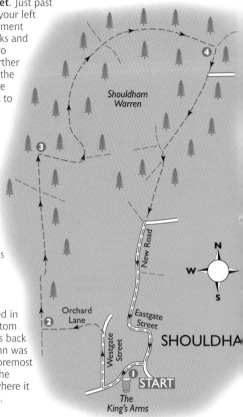

Shouldham Warren

New Road

Orchard Lane

Westgate Street

Eastgate Street

SHOULDHA

START

The King's Arms

Oxborough Hall

5 Oxborough

3¼ miles (5.2 km)

WALK HIGHLIGHTS

The name of this village is derived from the Old English for a fortified place frequented by oxen. In the Domesday Book it is listed as *Oxenburgh*. It lies in the heart of a peaceful and rural part of West Norfolk known as the Brecks.

St John the Evangelist Church stands opposite the Bedingfeld Arms, and would have looked complete, had it not been for the tower and spire crumbling one day in 1948; this event brought down the nave roof as well! The tower and nave areas are now grassed over, with the walls of the nave remaining upright. The only part to survive intact is the 16th-century chancel, which is famous for its terracotta tombs and tombstones, examples of the peak of Catholic art on the eve of the Reformation.

The Bedingfeld Arms pays homage to the family who are associated with Oxburgh Hall nearby. Dogs are welcome at this elegant and comfortable coaching inn, which has been serving customers since 1783.

Guide to Norfolk Pub Walks

HOW TO GET THERE AND PARKING: Turn off the A134 onto the Oxborough Road at Stoke Ferry. Drive into the village, turning right at the church; the pub is over the next road junction on the right. There is a car park at the front of the pub, but please ask the landlord before using it. **Sat nav** PE33 9PS.

MAP: OS Explorer 236 King's Lynn, Downham Market & Swaffham. **Grid Ref:** TF 744014.

THE PUB
The Bedingfeld Arms, PE33 9PS
☎ 01366 328300 www.bedingfeldarms.co.uk

THE WALK

1 From the **Bedingfeld Arms** car park, turn left to the crossroads, with **St John the Evangelist Church** adjacent to you. Turn right to the main road, and then cross over into **Eastmoor Road**; as you leave the village behind, the road affords expansive views of **Brecks** farmland. A hundred metres or so prior to the first houses since leaving the village, take a right turn at a footpath sign, which directs you diagonally across a field along a well-worn path. Head towards a point midway along the far edge of the field. Once there, cross over into the next field, again crossing diagonally to the right. The path should be fairly well defined. Once you are across this field, continue left along a sandy track lined by trees on your right.

2 After half a mile, the track turns sharp right towards **Caldecote Farm**. Turn right here onto the road. On the left are the earthworks of the Church of St Mary the Virgin, which was consecrated in the 16th century and became disused around 300 years later. Not much more of its history is known. Follow the road where it turns sharp right towards **Gooderstone** and **Oxborough**. At the crossroads, go straight over.

3 Just before the bridge over the **River Gadder**, go right over a stile. Cross another stile, and head towards the right-hand corner of the next meadow, where you'll cross a third stile. Veer to the right of the hedge ahead. Cross the track at the entrance to **Oxborough Fishing Lakes**, and continue along the path beside the field. After 150 metres, turn right over a stile around the backs of some houses. Turn left at the lane, and return to the pub.

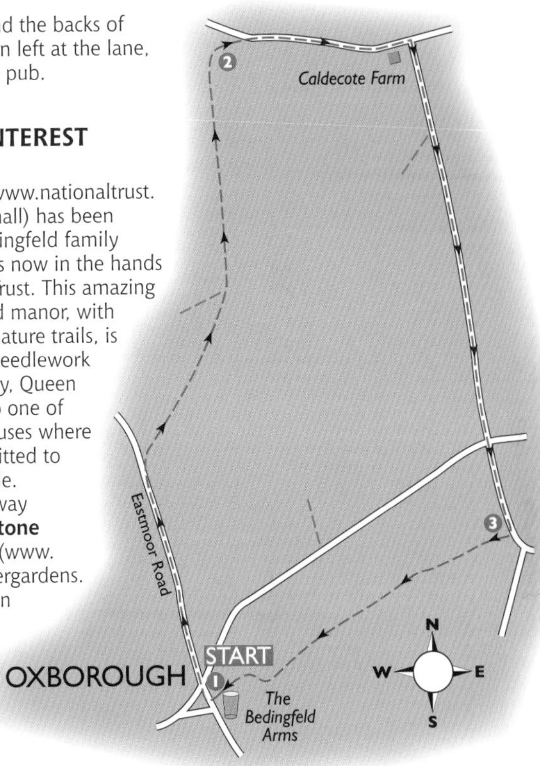

PLACES OF INTEREST NEARBY

Oxburgh Hall (www.nationaltrust. org.uk/oxburgh-hall) has been home to the Bedingfeld family since 1482 and is now in the hands of the National Trust. This amazing medieval moated manor, with its gardens and nature trails, is notable for the needlework hangings by Mary, Queen of Scots; it is also one of the few great houses where visitors are permitted to enter a priest hole.

A few miles away are the **Gooderstone Water Gardens** (www. gooderstonewatergardens. co.uk), created on six acres of land in the 1970s and restored to renewed beauty in 2003. A highlight is the Monet Pond, where lilies and willows are in abundance; you may see kingfishers from the bird hides.

Caldecote Farm

Eastmoor Road

OXBOROUGH START

The Bedingfeld Arms

Denver Sluice

6 Denver

2¼ miles (3.6 km)

WALK HIGHLIGHTS

A couple of miles from the charming village of Denver stands the impressive Denver Sluice complex, which is the modern successor to Vermuyden's, built in 1651. It was designed to defend the low-lying agricultural land of the Fens from the tidal surges of the River Great Ouse. The present-day sluice was constructed in 1834 by John Rennie and, with a few improvements, has stood the test of time well. This area is good for birdwatchers; in harsh winters, when other freshwater sites freeze over, the area in the vicinity of the sluice remains ice-free, attracting goosanders, smew, scaup, grebes and more.

THE PUB

The Jenyns Arms, PE38 0EQ

☎ 01366 383366   www.jenynsarms.com

HOW TO GET THERE AND PARKING: Turn off the A10 onto the Ely Road and then left onto Sluice Road. Cross the two main sluices; the road turns sharp left. The pub is on your left. If you're not visiting the pub, you can park in the free public car park near the sluice. **Sat nav PE38 0EQ.**

MAP: OS Explorer 236 King's Lynn, Downham Market & Swaffham. **Grid Ref:** TF 587009.

THE WALK

From the **Jenyns Arms**, go right, uphill and over **Denver Sluice**. At the other side of the sluice, turn left along the massive flood bank of the **River Great Ouse**, following the signpost for the **Fen Rivers Way**, the full length of which runs for nearly fifty miles, connecting the historic settlements of King's Lynn and Cambridge. Some 100 metres further on, you'll pass through a kissing gate and then continue along the riverbank. In this tranquil fenland landscape, look out for the wide variety of bird life. After about a mile, take a path down towards a lower embankment and across to a stile. Once

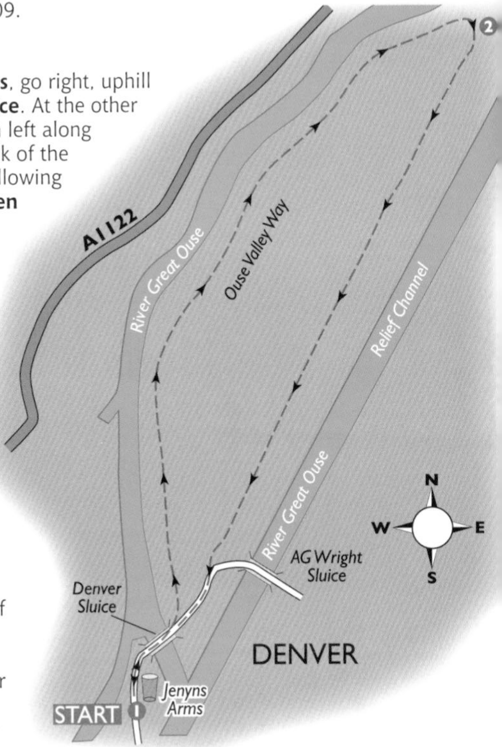

21

The Jenyns Arms

over the stile, head for the embankment ahead.

2 Turn right, and follow the bank of the **Relief Channel** towards the **A.G. Wright Sluice**. Pass through the kissing gate, turn right, and follow the road back to the pub.

PLACES OF INTEREST NEARBY

The Wildfowl and Wetlands Trust is responsible for the **Welney Wetland Centre** (www.wwt.org.uk/wetland-centres/welney), which is only a few miles away, set in the heart of the Fens. In the winter months, thousands of birds descend on the wetlands; you can watch the feeding of swans and other wildfowl from the centrally heated hide.

Brancaster Beach and The Royal West Norfolk Golf Club

7 Brancaster
4 miles (6.4 km)

WALK HIGHLIGHTS
Down on the wild marshes, ducks and geese winter along this section of coast in considerable numbers. At the beach, mile upon mile of unspoilt golden sand stretches away in both directions, with the added attraction of a shipwreck visible at low tide. These are the remains of the *SS Vina*, which was used by the RAF for target practice before the Normandy landings. She accidentally sank in 1944 after she dragged her anchor in a north-westerly gale and became marooned on one of the many sandbanks in the vicinity.

Locally caught mussels and seafood are the speciality of the Ship Hotel, which won prizes at the Norfolk Food and Drink Awards in 2014. You can relax next to the roaring wood burner in the chilly winter months.

THE PUB
The Ship Hotel, PE31 8AP
☎ 01485 210333 www.shiphotelnorfolk.co.uk

HOW TO GET THERE AND PARKING: Brancaster lies on the A149 coast road between Wells-next-the-Sea and Hunstanton. The pub sits opposite the church. Providing you use the pub, the landlord is happy for you to use the car park. **Sat nav** PE31 8AP.

MAP: OS Explorer 250 Norfolk Coast West. **Grid Ref:** TF 772438.

THE WALK

1 From the **Ship Hotel**, turn left along the coast road, and take the first turning left. After fifty metres, proceed right into **Choseley Road**, and keep heading inland on the **Norfolk Coast Path** for around three quarters of a mile. During this stretch, the path turns right and then left. Continue to the top of the hill. Turn right here still following the Norfolk Coast Path. Oddly enough, Brancaster was the first choice for Britain's equivalent of Cape Canaveral in the 1960s. The village could have been the launch site of a number of rockets, had it not been for the rise of oil rig installations in the North Sea that would have made the whole operation too dangerous.

2 After ¼ of a mile, look out for a gap in the hedge on the right and turn here onto a permissive footpath. There is a map of footpaths attached to a post here. Follow the path beside the hedge. Further down, the views over **Titchwell** village and the **Brancaster marshes** are spectacular. When you reach the coast road again, turn right and then immediately left along a tree-lined path that heads towards the sea. Once you are out of the wooded part of the footpath, keep following the path, with reed beds on both sides and dunes in the distance, along with salt marshes and intertidal mud flats. The path winds round to the right and then to the left. A hundred metres further on, take the path that goes straight ahead, down a slope and across a concrete pathway. Keep going until you reach **Brancaster beach**, a huge, wild and wide expanse of sand with big skies.

3 Turn right along the beach until you come to some granite sea defence blocks. Climb up the dunes here and onto the footpath, and turn left towards the large building of the **Royal West Norfolk Golf Clubhouse**, which stands defiantly against the roaring winds and lashing tides. Just before you come to the building, you need to go right along a raised bank for half a mile; the bank runs parallel with the road to **Brancaster**

village most of the way. At a T-junction of paths, turn left along a gravel track with houses on both sides. Turn right when you get to the road. Take the first left into **Butchers Lane**, and at the T-junction, turn right into **London Street** up to the main road. Turn right here, and walk back to the pub.

PLACES OF INTEREST NEARBY

For ornithologists, a visit to **RSPB Titchwell Marsh** (www.rspb.org.uk/Titchwell) is a must; it can be found by heading west along the coast road from Brancaster. The reserve contains reed beds, shallow lagoons and a sandy beach, and is home to avocets, marsh harriers and terns, to name a few. There is a well-stocked shop and café there, too.

To the east of Brancaster are the **Burnhams**, a group of villages of which Burnham Market and Burnham Thorpe are the most interesting. Burnham Market is a picturesque, vibrant and trendy place nicknamed 'Chelsea-on-Sea', whilst Burnham Thorpe is the birthplace of Horatio Nelson.

The village of Houghton St Giles at point 3 on the walk

8 **Little Walsingham**

4 miles (6.4 km)

WALK HIGHLIGHTS

In medieval times, Walsingham, often called the Nazareth of England, was one of the most visited pilgrimage sites in the world, but all that changed after the Reformation. In the nineteenth century, however, it began to regain some of its former glory, and nowadays, every year, thousands visit this little Norfolk village famous for its shrines in honour of the Virgin Mary.

Walsingham Abbey stands behind the facade of buildings on the corner to the left of the Bull Inn, as you look up the road. It has a long history of religious pilgrimage dating back to the eleventh century, and is famous for its spectacular ruins.

THE PUB

The Bull Inn, NR22 6BP

☎ 01328 820333 www.walsinghambull.co.uk

HOW TO GET THERE AND PARKING: From the A148 just outside Fakenham, take the B1105 to Wells and Walsingham. Where the B1105 turns left to Wells, keep straight on towards Little Walsingham. Drive through the village to the old village pump, situated on an island in the road. Turn left for the pay and display car park. (You turn right at the pump for the pub, but there is no parking there.) **Sat nav** NR22 6DH.

MAP: OS Explorer 251 Norfolk Coast Central. **Grid Ref:** TF 934368.

THE WALK

From the **Bull**, head up the road, past the village pump, and turn left into the **High Street**. If you've chosen to start the walk from the car park, return on foot the way you drove in, and turn right into the High Street. Take the first road right into **Friday Market**, veering right up **Station Road**. Pass the old railway station on your left, complete with a dome. This is now **St Seraphim's Orthodox Chapel**. At the road, go straight over between a pair of bollards and up a tree-lined tarmac path. When you reach the road junction, turn left; then, after

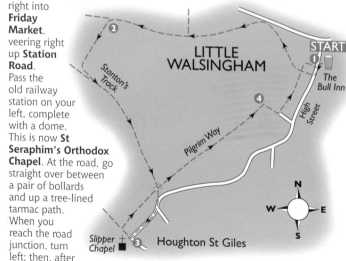

27

Guide to Norfolk Pub Walks

a few metres, turn left again along a footpath, and head straight on for three quarters of a mile, passing between some farm buildings on the way. Here you can take in commanding views of rolling Norfolk countryside; on a clear day, you may be able to view the sea to the north.

2 When the track bends left near an estate sign, take this track downhill. At the T-junction of paths, turn left along a stony path known as **Stanton's Track**. After nearly three quarters of a mile you'll pass under an old railway bridge; 100 metres beyond that, turn right onto a road heading towards the **Slipper Chapel**, the Catholic National Shrine of Our Lady of Walsingham. The small village of **Houghton St Giles** and its church will appear on your left. At the site of the Slipper Chapel, you'll find refreshments and toilets.

3 To return to Little Walsingham, take the concrete track opposite the chapel complex marked '**Pilgrim Way**'; after 100 metres, turn right onto the disused railway track. The Pilgrim Way used to run along the road back into the village, but this alternative route allows traffic-free access between the chapel and Little Walsingham.

4 When you come to the road near the coach park nearly a mile later, turn right, head downhill, and then turn first left into **Back Lane**. The remains of Walsingham Friary can be seen to the right further along this road. At the crossroads, head straight over. After 150 metres, turn right down **Swan Entry** to the **High Street**, where you turn left and then immediately right to arrive back at the pub.

PLACES OF INTEREST NEARBY

Just six miles away is **Langham Glass** (www.langhamglass.co.uk), where a team of glassmakers can be seen creating Langham's well-known handmade crystal.

The **Thursford Collection** (www.thursford.com) is a museum housing the world's largest collection of steam engines and organs, including a Mighty Wurlitzer, the fourth largest in the world, and a nineteenth-century gondola merry-go-round.

If you get a chance, **Holkham Bay**, with its unspoilt vista of pinewoods and mile upon mile of dunes and sandy beach, is also well worth a visit.

Great Hockham Woods

9 Great Hockham
4¼ miles (6.8 km)

WALK HIGHLIGHTS
Great Hockham, on the eastern border of Breckland, has a central, picture-postcard village green. The Forestry Commission acquired much of the surrounding heathland in the 1920s, and now more than half of the parish is woodland. The area is particularly renowned for its pingo ponds. These were formed at the end of the last ice age when temperatures rose, melting lenses of ice in the ground. Great Hockham is also mentioned in the Domesday Book. Dog owners will be more than welcome at the Eagle, which is featured in *CAMRA's Good Beer Guide 2017*.

THE PUB
The Eagle, IP24 1NP
☎ 01953 498893 www.hockhameagle.com

Guide to Norfolk Pub Walks

HOW TO GET THERE AND PARKING: Great Hockham is off the A1075, between Watton and Thetford. Take the Wretham Road; as you come into the village, turn right, and the Eagle is on the next corner. Parking is available at the side of the pub, but check with the landlord first as a courtesy. **Sat nav** IP24 1NP.

MAP: OS Explorer 237 Norwich. **Grid Ref:** TL 953924.

THE WALK

1 Turn right out of the **Eagle** pub towards the **Great Hockham** sign on the village green at the crossroads. Head straight over, signposted to **Watton**, past a mix of old and new dwellings. After 200 metres, turn left along **Vicarage Road**, a quiet lane leading away from the village. At the main road, cross straight over towards **West Farm**. Just before the gate leading to the farmhouse and outbuildings, turn right along a track. After half a mile, you'll enter **Great Hockham Woods**, owned by the Forestry Commission. Head straight along the main footpath until you reach a crossroads of paths.

2 Turn left here, and when you reach the lane, turn left again. When the road bends round to the right, carry straight on along a no through road. Passing a left-hand turn into a campsite, the road narrows into a small footpath before emerging on the main road. Cross over here, and walk down a track signposted 'Peddars Way Bridle Route' for three quarters of a mile. It begins as a wooded trail and then opens out, offering fine views across the farmland towards **Little Hockham**.

3 Turn left, and proceed along a wide, hedged path, signposted '**Wildlife Trail**' and '**Public Footpath**'. When you reach the farm outbuildings in Little Hockham, turn left, and follow the lane. Towards the end of this lane, you'll pass the grounds of **Hockham Hall** on the left. The last part of the lane was diverted in the eighteenth century: the owner of the Hall did not want people passing his house. At the T-junction, turn left, and the Eagle is on your right.

PLACES OF INTEREST NEARBY

On the Norfolk–Suffolk border stands **Thetford**, one of the largest towns in Norfolk. Thomas Paine, the author of *Rights of Man*, was born here.

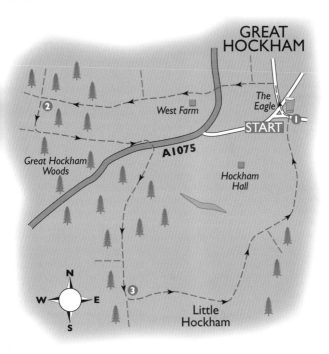

Thetford hosts the **Dad's Army Museum** (www.dadsarmythetford.org. uk) and, nearby, the **English Whisky Company** at Roudham (www. englishwhisky.co.uk), where you can take a tour of the distillery, learn how the whisky is made in their beautiful copper stills, and taste one or two famous malts.

The beach at Cley next the Sea

10 Cley next the Sea

3½ miles (5.6 km)

WALK HIGHLIGHTS

Norfolk is home to some of the most outstanding birdwatching spots in the UK, and the Norfolk Wildlife Trust's Cley Marshes has often been championed as the premier site. It was built specifically as a bird-breeding nature reserve, and boasts 400 acres of marsh with an eco-friendly visitor centre, observation area, café and shop. The views across the marshes from the observation area are breathtaking. Large numbers of wintering and migrating wildfowl and waders, as well as bitterns and marsh harriers, are attracted to the reed beds, shingle beach, grazing marsh and saline lagoons.

Cley is one of the most picturesque villages on the North Norfolk coast, with narrow streets, flint houses and an array of independent shops. It's well worth spending some time exploring the charms of this coastal village.

The George Hotel is dog-friendly, and will welcome you with a roaring open fire on chillier days and a large beer garden in the summer.

HOW TO GET THERE AND PARKING: Cley next the Sea is situated on the main A149 coast road between Sheringham and Wells-next-the-Sea. The George Hotel lies on the same road in the village. There is parking on the street outside the hotel. **Sat nav** NR25 7RN.

MAP: OS Explorer 251 Norfolk Coast Central. **Grid Ref:** TG 044439.

THE PUB
The George Hotel, NR25 7RN
☎ 01263 740652 www.thegeorgehotelatcley.co.uk

THE WALK
From the coast road outside the **George Hotel**, turn left; after 100 metres, just before the **Old Town Hall House**, proceed right down a narrow alleyway, then right again around the back of the houses on the **High Street** and on to **Cley windmill**. Go beyond the windmill, following a sign marked '**Cley Beach Coast Path**' through a gate and then up and down some steps onto a path beside some reed beds. Follow the path round and up onto a raised path, and then take the lower of the two raised paths, signposted '**National Trail**' and heading away from Cley itself. Follow this path towards the sea, eventually running parallel with the road leading to the beach car park.

At the beach, turn right, following the **Norfolk Coast Path** signs. After three quarters of a mile, take a right turn onto a raised path through the marshes. There are amazing views to either side of this wildlife sanctuary, which is a paradise for ornithologists.

Just before the main road, turn right down a set of steps, and continue along the path running parallel with the coast road. Further along on the left, look out for Norfolk Wildlife Trust's **Cley Marshes visitor centre** and car park. Tickets can be obtained here for the reserve itself. Keep straight on, and follow the path. When you reach a path off to the right to the bird hides, turn left across a wooden bridge to the coast road. Cross the road, turn left, and walk for about 100 metres.

Turn right into the cul-de-sac **Hilltop**. When you have nearly reached the end of Hilltop, turn right down a footpath with sweeping views over the marshes. At the bottom of the hill, turn left along a rough track. Two hundred metres past the **High Street** sign, follow a footpath to the left between high flint walls, signposted to the car park and village centre. When you reach the road, turn left; after 100 metres, turn right down a path signposted to the village centre.

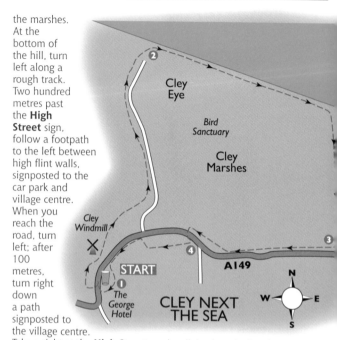

Take a right at the **High Street**, and walk back to the hotel.

PLACES OF INTEREST NEARBY

Beans Boats (www.beansboattrips.co.uk) operate trips from Morston quay, to the west of Cley. They offer a trip on one of their licensed ferries to see the **seal colony at Blakeney Point**, which is also one of the most important sites in Europe for migrating birds. Situated on the coast road out of Cley towards Blakeney, meanwhile, is **The Barn at Artemis** (www.thebarnatartemis.co.uk). This is a great little shop to browse in; it contains clothing, antiques, fragrances and homeware.

Weybourne Windmill

11 Weybourne
4¼ miles (6.8 km)

WALK HIGHLIGHTS
This walk covers one of the main areas of outstanding scenic beauty on the North Norfolk coast, and is wonderfully varied, passing through woods, heathland, fields, parkland and along a clifftop. The Sheringham Shoal wind farm catches the eye out to sea, with over eighty wind turbines providing green energy day and night.

Weybourne Station was originally opened in 1901 as part of the Midland and Great Northern Joint Railway, with the idea of developing Weybourne as a holiday resort. Sadly, this never took off, and the railway's fate was sealed in 1964. In 1975, however, the station was reopened as part of the North Norfolk Railway, or 'Poppy Line', a heritage steam railway.

The Ship Inn invites you to sample the seafood caught at the local beach and to cosy up to the log burner on cold wintry days.

THE PUB
The Ship Inn, NR25 7SZ
☎ 01263 588721 www.theshipinnweybourne.com

HOW TO GET THERE AND PARKING: Weybourne sits to the north-east of Holt on the A149 coast road between Sheringham and Cley next the Sea. The Ship Inn can be found in the centre of the village on this road. The car park, at the side of the pub, has very limited space, but you can also park on the roads nearby. **Sat nav NR25 7SZ.**

MAP: OS Explorer 252 Norfolk Coast East. **Grid Ref:** TG 110430.

THE WALK

1 From the **Ship Inn** car park, turn right and then right again into **Church Street**, then left into **Station Road**. Follow the road uphill to **Weybourne Station**, on the famous 'Poppy Line'.

2 If the station is open, you can cross the footbridge over the railway line. Under the footbridge is a way out from the platform onto a grass path. Turn left onto this path. (If the station is closed, cross the railway bridge, and then turn left down the footpath.) Follow the path, passing to the right of a closed gate, and carry on straight ahead, ignoring the path to the right. Continue along this path, which borders the conifer wood of **Weybourne Heath**. From here, there are magnificent views of **Weybourne Windmill** and of the wind farm off the coast. The path veers to the left and then to the right, and continues, cutting through part of the heath itself. Where the path forks, take the left-hand way through the trees, and follow the path downhill into the National Trust's **Sheringham Park**, well known for its blaze of colour in late May from the prolific number of azalea and rhododendron bushes throughout its length and breadth. From the Sheringham Park sign, the path wends uphill until you come to a T-junction of paths.

3 Turn left, signposted '**Coastal Path**'. On this path are signs to the gazebo, which is well worth a visit. It is a high tower that offers panoramic views across the Norfolk coast and Sheringham Park itself. At the A149, cross straight over, and follow the footpath along the edge of the field. Once you pass through the hedge, turn left, heading towards the North Sea and crossing a railway bridge en route.

4 As you approach the cliffs, veer left along the clifftop, heading towards a row of terraced houses. Listen out for the song of the skylarks, who can be seen and heard on the cliff all year round. As you near the houses, which get precariously closer to the cliff edge each year, pass through a gate, and turn left up the track. Just past the houses, turn right through the hedge and through a gate, and head on along the clifftop again

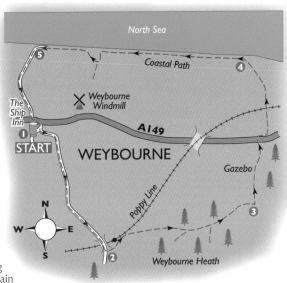

towards **Weybourne beach**. The path descends to the beach, where sea angling is very popular.

Turn left up the road to **Weybourne village**. At the T-junction, turn left, and walk back to the pub.

PLACES OF INTEREST NEARBY

The National Trust's **Sheringham Park** is a stunning park with gardens, landscaped by the designer Humphrey Repton. In May and June, the park is awash with vivid colours from the eighty or so species of azaleas and rhododendrons. Whilst Sheringham Hall itself is a private residence, the park has over a thousand acres open to the public to explore.

The Kings Arms in Reepham

12 Reepham
4¼ miles (6.8 km)

WALK HIGHLIGHTS
This beautiful walk takes in the market town of Reepham, a disused railway, rural country paths, fields and meadows, quiet lanes and waterways. Reepham itself is one of the finest market towns in Norfolk, with many eighteenth-century houses; many of those around the Market Place demonstrate Flemish influence. This walk also showcases the impressive countryside between the Bure and Wensum Valleys.

THE PUB
The Kings Arms, NR10 4JJ
☎ 01603 870345   www.kingsarmsreepham.com

THE WALK
1 As you face into the car park from the entrance, head right and then left at a garden wall to walk along a short alley and down to some railings. Turn right along **Chapel Walk**, which leads into **Fishers Alley**; this, in turn, leads into the **Market Place**, and you'll see the **Kings Arms** as you emerge. From the pub, pass the library on your right, and then turn right into **Church Hill**. On your right is **St Michael's Church**. Proceed left at the convenience stores along **Ollands Road** for a third of a mile, passing the **Crown** pub and arriving at the T-junction with the

HOW TO GET THERE AND PARKING: The B1145 runs through Reepham from Bawdeswell to Cawston. Once you reach the town, turn left at the crossroads to stay on the B1145; the car park is on the right. For the pub, walk back to the crossroads and into the Market Place to find the Kings Arms in the southern corner. **Sat nav** NR10 4LF.

MAP: OS Explorer 238 Dereham and Aylsham. **Grid Ref:** TG 099229.

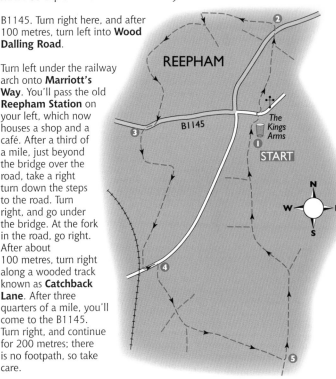

B1145. Turn right here, and after 100 metres, turn left into **Wood Dalling Road**.

Turn left under the railway arch onto **Marriott's Way**. You'll pass the old **Reepham Station** on your left, which now houses a shop and a café. After a third of a mile, just beyond the bridge over the road, take a right turn down the steps to the road. Turn right, and go under the bridge. At the fork in the road, go right. After about 100 metres, turn right along a wooded track known as **Catchback Lane**. After three quarters of a mile, you'll come to the B1145. Turn right, and continue for 200 metres; there is no footpath, so take care.

3 Turn left on the road bend onto a lane with a '**No Through Road**' sign. Follow the lane as it turns sharp left and leads onto a grassy footpath. After just over 200 metres, turn right before the school playing fields, and keep to this path for about half a mile. At the end of the path, turn left onto the road, passing the **Whitwell and Reepham Railway** on your right.

4 At the top of the hill, proceed right, following the signpost to **Whitwell Campsite** along a hedged track with good views over the Wensum Valley. Veer left after the campsite, keeping to the wooded footpath with overhanging trees. At the road junction, continue straight ahead, following the signpost to **Little Witchingham and Great Witchingham**. After around 200 metres, turn left after the bridge at **Eades Mill**, and head uphill.

5 When you reach the T-junction, turn left onto **Furze Lane**, signposted to **Cawston and Booton**. Follow this road for 700 metres, passing Manor Farmhouse on the left, until you reach a public footpath sign on the left. Take the footpath, passing through some woodland and then over a wooden bridge over a stream. Climb the stile, and head towards the house. Climb over the next stile, turn right, and continue straight ahead, following the lane. Where the lane turns sharp left, keep straight on into **Bar Lane**, heading towards the church. You'll pass school playing fields on your left on the way. Keep straight on past the houses. At the end of the path, where there is an arch overhead, turn right along **Church Street** past the **Town Hall**, and then turn left into the churchyard. Turn left at the church, and head towards the **Market Place**. Keep straight on, and then turn left for the pub.

PLACES OF INTEREST NEARBY

Gressenhall Farm and Workhouse (www.museums.norfolk.gov.uk/gressenhall-farm-and-workhouse) gives an insight into the conditions of the old workhouses and life on the land.

Looking back to Ringland from Royal Hill

13 Ringland
2½ miles (4 km)

WALK HIGHLIGHTS

Ringland is a small village nestling in the Wensum Valley. In the summer, the grassy area leading down to the River Wensum in front of the pub is a magnet for picnickers, paddlers and canoeists. The river is shallow here, and a lovely spot to immerse oneself in the beauty of Norfolk's rural landscape.

The large Church of St Peter dates back to the fifteenth century, and the rich, vaulted timber roof is said to be one of the finest in East Anglia. The clerestory houses what is considered to be one of central Norfolk's finest collections of late medieval stained glass.

THE PUB
The Swan Inn, NR8 6AB
☎ 01603 869014   www.ringlandswan.co.uk

THE WALK

From the **Swan Inn** car park, turn left onto the road past the pub, and turn left, signposted to the village hall and the church. Continue for half a mile through the village until you reach the large **Church of St**

Guide to Norfolk Pub Walks

HOW TO GET THERE AND PARKING: At the roundabout at Easton on the A47, turn off towards Ringland Hills, and follow the winding lane to a T-junction. Turn left, follow the river, and the pub is on your left. There is ample parking at the side of the pub, but please check with the landlord first. If you order your meal before you start the walk, it will be ready on your return. **Sat nav** NR8 6AB.

MAP: OS Explorer 238 Dereham & Aylsham. **Grid Ref:** TG 139139.

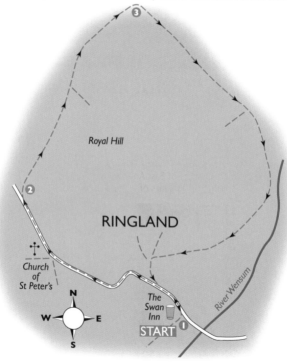

Peter's. Turn right here along **The Street** (formerly Longrow Lane) for 350 metres.

Turn right onto a dirt track, and follow it up what is known as **Royal Hill**; from the top of the hill, you'll catch great views of the **Wensum Valley**. Head down towards the isolated house. Pass to the right of it, and then through a gate.

Turn immediately right, and follow the hedge. At this point, you are on a level with the wonderfully scenic water meadows and the **River Wensum**. When you see a gate on your right, go through it and take the tree-lined footpath. This path gives way to a larger track further along. At the **Back Lane** road sign, veer left and down to the green and the village sign. Turn left here, and follow the road back to the **Swan**.

PLACES OF INTEREST NEARBY

The city of **Norwich** is well worth a visit, the main attractions being the permanent market, the cathedral, the castle and the historic Lanes district, along with the many shopping attractions. Tombland and Elm Hill, both close to the cathedral, boast some of the best independent shops and cafés in Norwich.

The **Sainsbury Centre for Visual Arts** (www.scva.ac.uk) is located on the campus of the University of East Anglia and is an inspirational public art museum, spanning 5,000 years of human creativity.

The Swan

The Burston Crown

14 Burston

3¼ miles (5.2 km)

WALK HIGHLIGHTS

This is a beautiful walk that takes you through rolling South Norfolk countryside, including woods, meadows and fields. The popular Burston Crown was voted Norfolk Pub of the Year in 2016, and is a great place to relax and sample good food and local ales in a comfortable and friendly environment. Open fires are ready to welcome you on cold winter days.

THE PUB

The Burston Crown, IP22 5TW
☎ 01379 741257 www.burstoncrown.com

THE WALK

1 From the front of the **Burston Crown**, turn left down the pub's gravel drive to the road, where you turn left again. After 100 metres or so, you'll see the local primary school on your right. Beyond the playground, turn right along a public footpath, and keep straight on until you reach a gate and a stile. Head for the telegraph pole in the middle of the field, and

HOW TO GET THERE AND PARKING: Burston lies off the A140 Norwich–Diss road. Drive through Shimpling, and past Burston Primary School, and the pub is on your right along a gravel driveway. Parking is available at the front of the pub, but it would be best to ask the landlord first. **Sat nav** IP22 5TW.

MAP: OS Explorer 230 Diss & Harleston. **Grid Ref:** TM 137832.

then for the gap in the hedge beyond that. Once through the gap, keep close to the hedge on your left, and follow it down to a stile in the corner of the field. Proceed across a small bridge and round the back of a house, and then turn right down a gravel driveway to a road. Turn left at the road.

After a few metres, turn right, and keep going straight ahead along a delightful path between undulating fields. After around 800 metres, this path enters into a wood. Once over the stile and clear of the wood,

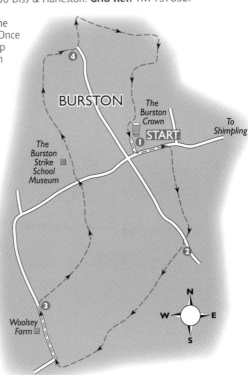

keep to the edge of the field – do not go diagonally across – and walk ound to an iron gate and another stile. Turn right at the road, and pass **Woolsey Farm** on the left.

3 After 150 metres, just before you reach a house on your right, turn right onto a footpath. Keep to the edge of the field. The path soon turns into a track between two hedges and then runs past some houses to a road. Turn left at the road, and after a few metres, turn right along a tree-lined track next to some small fields with animals. After half a mile, you'll come to bigger agricultural units on your right; at the T-junction, turn right.

4 At the next T-junction, turn left past some industrial units. After nearly 200 metres, turn right down a footpath through an avenue of trees and over a small bridge. Keep following the path through a copse. At a T-junction of paths, turn right and then left towards and then through another copse. At another T-junction of paths, turn right and then immediately left over another small bridge. At this point, proceed straight ahead over the field, which may be muddy in the winter months. Once you are over this field, turn right before the ditch, and with the hedge on your left, follow the edge of the field along to a sharp right turn at the end of the field. Then, after 250 metres, turn left, and follow the hedge round to your right, with the hedge on your right now. Continue to follow the edge of the field as it winds round for about 600 metres until you come to a small bridge. Turn right over the bridge and then through a metal link stile. Head straight across the paddock to another metal link stile on the other side. Follow the path round past some houses and back to the **Burston Crown**.

PLACES OF INTEREST NEARBY

The **Burston Strike School Museum** is a stone's throw to the west of the Burston Crown and can easily be reached on foot. The museum chronicles the longest strike in British history, which occurred in Burston. It ran from 1914 until 1939, and started after two teachers, who were at odds with the ruling class of the local management committee, were sacked. A strike was announced, with parents and children siding with the teachers.

Blickling Hall

15 Blickling
3½ miles (5.6 km)

WALK HIGHLIGHTS
Much of this walk connects with the Weavers' Way, a sixty-one-mile route of amazing diversity that links Cromer with Great Yarmouth. On the way, you will pass the site of Blickling Mill, though there is nothing to suggest the three-storey working mill that once towered over the landscape here. It is thought that it was rebuilt for the final time in 1779, but due to age and neglect, the two upper storeys were removed around 1930. The remaining buildings were renovated and are the only remains of the mill that survive today.

On the latter part of the walk, you'll see the Tower, which was built in the grounds of Blickling Hall in the 1770s as a grandstand; the racecourse used to stand in the field now known as Tower Park. Of the 4,600 acres of the Blickling Estate, 950 acres consist of woodland and parkland. This is a particularly tranquil stretch, with grazing animals, abundant birdsong and that big Norfolk sky!

THE PUB
The Buckinghamshire Arms, NR11 6NF
☎ 01263 732133 www.bucksarms.co.uk

HOW TO GET THERE AND PARKING: Blickling can be reached from the A140 Norwich–Cromer road by turning off at the Aylsham roundabout, driving into Aylsham and following the signs to Blickling Hall. Veer right just after Blickling Hall, and the pub is on your left. There is a pub car park, but check with the landlord first as a courtesy. Further parking is available close by in the National Trust car park, where a fee applies for non-members. **Sat nav** NR11 6NF.

MAP: OS Explorer 252 Norfolk Coast East. **Grid Ref:** TG 178286.

THE WALK

1 Turn left from the **Buckinghamshire Arms** along the **Weavers' Way**. Take the second right-hand fork, and go through the white gate into **Blickling Park**. Continue straight ahead, still keeping to the Weavers' Way. On your right, you'll notice the large ornamental lake. As you approach a belt of trees, you'll pass through a second gate. After 100 metres, you leave the Weavers' Way and continue straight along a narrower path towards the hamlet of **Moorgate**.

2 Turn left at the lane, and follow the road for one and a quarter miles until you reach the National Trust woodland car park on your left. During this section of the walk, you'll pass the site of the old **Blickling Mill** on the **River Bure**.

3 In the car park, take the track round the five-bar gate, and head along the well-worn track. As you walk up this track, you'll catch sight of the Tower on your right. Keep heading straight on. At a T-junction of paths, turn right.

4 After fifty metres or so, turn left through a small wooden gate, and follow the path with the lake to your left and **Blickling Hall** straight ahead. As the path veers left to face the lake, take the path to the right towards the house. Just before you reach the fence, turn right, heading towards a wooden gate. Pass through the gate with the walled garden on your left. At the end of the wall, turn left and walk back to the Buckinghamshire Arms.

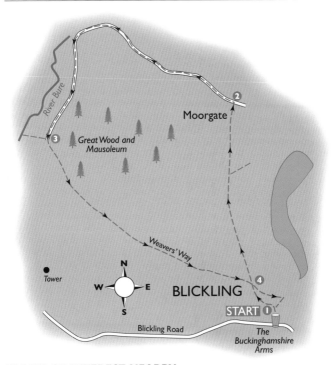

PLACES OF INTEREST NEARBY

A magnificent Jacobean stately home, with parkland, a lake and gardens set in the beautiful Bure meadows, **Blickling Hall** (www.nationaltrust.org. uk/blickling-estate) is well worth a visit. The estate was once owned by the Boleyn family; Anne, the ill-fated wife of Henry VIII, was born here, and it is said that her ghost appears in the grounds! The **Bure Valley Railway** (www.bvrw.co.uk) runs the 18-mile round trip from the historic market town of Aylsham to the capital of the Norfolk Broads at Wroxham. You can hop off and back on at any station, giving you time to explore the area.

The Vernon Arms

16 Southrepps

5¾ miles (9.3 km)

WALK HIGHLIGHTS

This is a beautiful walk connecting Southrepps with Northrepps and taking in some of the most striking rural aspects of Norfolk. The Vernon Arms is a great example of a welcoming and friendly village hostelry. It serves good food and ales, and is a perfect place to relax and enjoy the atmosphere around a log fire in the winter months.

THE PUB

The Vernon Arms, NR11 8NP
☎ 01263 833355 www.vernonarms.com

THE WALK

1 From the **Vernon Arms** car park, turn right up **Church Street** towards **St James Church**. Turn right at the church. Follow the road round to your left. After around half a mile, the road turns sharply to the right; turn left through some white gates at this point. At the end of this path, you'll pass through some more white gates. At the road, cross over and keep going straight on. The grass path changes to a gravel track, which goes past some houses. At the lane, turn right.

2 At the T-junction, cross straight over the road and onto a footpath. At a T-junction of paths, turn left; at the next T-junction of paths, turn left again.

HOW TO GET THERE AND PARKING: Southrepps stands to the east of Roughton, which is on the A140 Norwich–Cromer road. Take the B1436 from Roughton, driving across the A149 and then into Southrepps village. The Vernon Arms is along this road on the left. Parking is available at the pub for those eating or drinking there, or on the streets nearby. **Sat nav** NR11 8NP.

MAP: OS Explorer 252 Norfolk Coast East. **Grid Ref:** TG 256365.

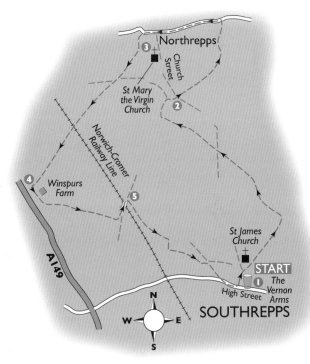

Just along here on the right is the supposedly haunted **Shrieking Pit**, a largish pond overhung by trees. Pass some farm buildings, and you'll reach a road, where you turn left. Follow the road down into **Northrepps**. At the bottom of the hill, continue ahead past the **Foundry Arms** on your left. A hundred metres or so past the pub, turn left into **Church Street**, and continue until you reach **St Mary the Virgin Church** on your right.

3 Turn right into the churchyard, signposted to Southrepps; then turn immediately left, following the gravel path. At the main church door, carry on straight ahead across the grass towards a gate. Pass through the gate, and follow the path towards Southrepps. Follow the signs along the edge of the field, enter a wood past a flint wall, and then turn right onto a wider track. After 80 metres, turn left at a footpath sign – it may be hidden by the undergrowth in the summer – and take the indicated path, which cuts through the middle of the field. At the end of the field, climb a stile, and go up some steps to the Norwich–Cromer railway line. Take care as you cross the railway tracks. Once you are over the next stile, keep straight on, and follow the path for around half a mile.

4 As you near **Winspurs Farm**, turn left, keeping the hedge on your left. Follow the path round the edge of the field. When the path comes to a T-junction, turn left, and keep straight on. When you reach the road, turn left, and pass over the railway bridge.

5 Turn immediately right, following the footpath signs. At a T-junction of paths, turn right. After 100 metres, you'll come to a footpath sign pointing left through the middle of a field towards a church. Take this path. Once over this field, you'll pass through a hedge and then go diagonally across the next field through a narrow alleyway. Then turn left, and follow the tarmac road. After a short distance, turn right, and keep going until the staggered junction; then turn left into the **High Street**, and walk back to the pub.

PLACES OF INTEREST NEARBY

Felbrigg Hall (www.nationaltrust.org.uk/felbrigg-hall-gardens-and-estate), now owned by the National Trust, has a long and interesting history, and is known for its Jacobean architecture and superb Georgian interior. Explore the house and gardens, along with 520 acres of woods, parkland and a lake.

Honing Lock

17 **East Ruston**
3¼ miles (5.2 km)

WALK HIGHLIGHTS
Honing Lock gives a glimpse of Norfolk's one and only artificial, locked, sailing waterway, the North Walsham and Dilham Canal. It runs for just under nine miles from Antingham to Wayford Bridge, where it connects to the navigable River Ant. Its six locks ascend the fifty-eight foot rise to Antingham, and were large enough to accommodate the cargo-carrying wherries. A good proportion of this walk is along the Weavers' Way, and this section follows the old railway line, which was originally owned by the Midland and Great Northern Joint Railway. The Weavers' Way is a sixty-one-mile walk that connects Cromer to Great Yarmouth and crosses a number of magnificent habitats and landscapes.

THE PUB
The Butchers Arms, NR12 9JG
☎ 01692 650237 No website

HOW TO GET THERE AND PARKING: From Stalham, travel north for about two and a half miles, taking the Brumstead Road and then the B1159. Take a left turn, following a sign to Honing and East Ruston, and follow the road for one and a quarter miles. The Butchers Arms is on your left, with a car park at the front. **Sat nav** NR12 9JG.

MAP: OS Explorer OL40 The Broads. **Grid Ref:** TG 345281.

THE WALK

1 Looking out from the pub, turn left across the car park, and follow a hedge- and tree-lined footpath. When you reach the road, turn right; after around 150 metres, turn left onto a grassy footpath, and follow the edge of the field. When you pass through a hedge, turn right, and follow the edge of another field. When you reach the road, turn right; after 150 metres or so, turn left around a double bend with views of undulating farmland in the distance. After 100 metres, turn right through a break in the hedgerow, and walk diagonally across the field towards a gap in

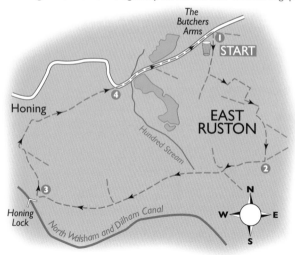

the hedge with a large barn behind it. Once through the gap, you head straight for a stile in the distance. Cross over, and walk round beside a barn and down towards an iron gate, where there's another stile.

Turn right towards **Honing and Worstead** along **Chapel Road**, which is dotted with cottages overlooking the meadows and paddocks which spread out from the lane. After just over 250 metres, turn left into the **Weavers' Way car park**, and walk up onto an old disused railway, which forms part of the Weavers' Way. Turn right here, and continue for a mile along a glorious stretch to Honing Lock. Along the way, pass through the first gate and go straight ahead, passing the **East Ruston Angling Club**; later on, you pass a stabling block on your left.

At the next gate, turn right. (If you turn left here and then right, heading downhill, you'll hear the rushing waters of the North Walsham and Dilham Canal's **Honing Lock**. Although this lock is in a state of disrepair, some parts of this unique Norfolk waterway are now being restored.) Continue uphill along the road. At the T-junction, turn left, and then turn right, signposted to **East Ruston**. After 250 metres, turn right to **Bush Farm**. After fifty metres, turn left onto a footpath across the field. Once you have crossed this field, you then cross a small bridge; head diagonally left across the next field and then across the third field towards the gap in the hedge, and walk down the steps.

At the road, turn right, and continue along this road all the way back to the pub on the right.

PLACES OF INTEREST NEARBY

Old Vicarage Gardens (www.e-ruston-oldvicaragegardens.co.uk) stands a mile or so away from the Butchers Arms, at the crossroads with the B1159. The owners started the garden from scratch fifteen years ago, and with much dedication and creativity have turned this corner of Norfolk into one of the 'must see' gardens of the county. One of the iconic landmarks of Norfolk, meanwhile, is the **Happisburgh Lighthouse**, painted white with three red bands. It is the oldest working light in East Anglia.

Farmland on the walk

18 Ludham

5½ miles (8.9 km)

WALK HIGHLIGHTS

Ludham is an appealing Broadland village surrounded on three sides by the Rivers Ant, Bure and Thurne. It stands at the end of a dyke leading to Womack Water. This walk takes you on a gloriously scenic route through the Ant Valley, with some breathtaking views. On the way, you'll pass How Hill, an imposing house built in 1904 as a holiday home for a Norwich architect. It has a commanding view over the River Ant and the surrounding marshes, and stands in an idyllic location. Today it is owned by the How Hill Trust, an environmental education charity.

THE PUB

The Kings Arms, NR29 5QQ
☎ 01692 678386 www.kingsarmsludham.co.uk

HOW TO GET THERE AND PARKING: Ludham stands on the A1062, which runs from Hoveton to Potter Heigham. The Kings Arms is right in the centre of the village. Parking is available at the side of the pub, but please enquire first. **Sat nav** NR29 5QQ.

MAP: OS Explorer OL40 The Broads. **Grid Ref:** TG 388183.

THE WALK

Turn right out of the **Kings Arms**, and take the left-hand turn down **Staithe Road**. After a third of a mile, turn right down **Lovers Lane**. This lane turns into a grassy track. Veer right at the fork.

At the crossroads, turn left from Lovers Lane onto the A1062. Just before the footpath ends near **Ludham Village Hall**, you'll see a gap in the hedge on the opposite side of the road. Go through this, and then walk

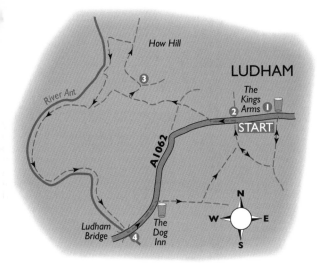

diagonally across the field. Once you've traversed the field, go through the gap in the hedge and walk diagonally across the next field. At the hedge in front of you, turn left, keeping the hedge on your right. After a short distance, go through the gap in the hedge, and then turn left, following a concrete path for a short while before veering left onto a narrow footpath leading to the road. Cross here into **Turf Fen Lane**. After a third of a mile, before the thatched house on your right, turn right onto a path, and go through a small gate. Follow the footpath around, through a meadow, over a bridge and through a gap in an overhanging hedge.

3 Turn left onto the road. You'll pass the entrance to **How Hill National Nature Reserve**; at the mill on your right, turn left past the **How Hill Study Centre**, and walk down to the **River Ant**. The views of the river and the marshes, complete with the odd windmill here and there, are spectacular. At the river, turn left past the moorings, and take the river path, which will veer to the left, away from the river itself. Continue past the reed beds on your right, and at the fork, turn sharp right along the raised path, taking you back in the direction of the river. Later, you'll pass through a gate and then onwards to **Ludham Bridge**, where there is a general stores selling, among other things, drinks and ice creams!

4 Turn left at Ludham Bridge along the road. After the **Dog Inn**, turn right down a lane signposted to **Hall Common**. After a third of a mile, the driveway to **Ludham Hall** will appear on the left. Turn left up this driveway, going between the hall on the left and some barns on the right. Continue along this track until you get to a fork; here, turn right into **Lovers Lane** and retrace your steps. The grass track gives way to a tarmac road. Turn left at the T-junction, walk along **Staithe Road**, and continue back to the pub.

PLACES OF INTEREST NEARBY
Fairhaven Woodland and Water Garden (www.fairhavengarden. co.uk) boasts 130 acres of ancient woodland and water gardens, with views over its own private broad. Enjoy the boat trips, gift shop and tea room, or just browse for plants.

Railway swing bridge and Norton Marshes

19 Reedham

3¾ miles (6 km)

WALK HIGHLIGHTS

The charming riverside village of Reedham stands on the north bank of the River Yare. Before the marshes towards Great Yarmouth were drained, Reedham was a coastal village with a Roman lighthouse. There has been a railway swing bridge here since 1847, when the Lowestoft line was built, but the present construction dates back to the early twentieth century, when the track was doubled in size. A swing bridge was preferred because it allowed wherries to pass through, whereas normal bridges were too low. Views over the surrounding miles of marshes dominate this walk, with the ever-present River Yare bringing holidaymakers and day trippers to sample the delights of life on the water.

HOW TO GET THERE AND PARKING: It is a rather circuitous route to Reedham, with no clear direct route to the village. Turn off the A47 at the B1140, and follow it for just over a mile. Turn left onto Sandy Lane, follow it for a mile, and continue onto Ash Tree Road, which leads onto the Reedham Road. Follow the signs for Freethorpe and Reedham. Once you are in Reedham, head for the river; the Lord Nelson is situated on the quay. Roadside parking is available along the quay. **Sat nav** NR13 3TE.

MAP: OS Explorer OL40 The Broads. **Grid Ref:** TG 419017.

THE PUB
The Lord Nelson, NR13 3TE
☎ 01493 700367 www.lordnelsonpub.com

THE WALK

1 From the **Lord Nelson**, turn right along **Reedham Quay** beside the **River Yare**. This quay was once the home of the local boatbuilding industry, with several wherries built here. The quay now supports a couple of pubs, some riverside cottages and a post office and shop. Follow the road uphill to the war memorial, turn left into **Station Road**, and follow the road round a sharp right-hand bend. On the left, across the marshes near the **Reedham Ferry** pub, is the Reedham Ferry itself, which is the only crossing on the Yare between Norwich and Great Yarmouth; a ferry has helped travellers cross the river here since the seventeenth century, and even today, using it saves a journey of around thirty miles. As you proceed along Station Road, just before the T-junction, turn right up the hill beside the railway station. Turn right at the T-junction with **Witton Green**, and follow the road to its end.

2 At this point, turn right along a path beside a field, and keep straight ahead. At the end of this path, there is a splendid panoramic view of the river, with **Norton Marshes** in the distance. Turn left at the road, and keep going until the second crossroads. Go straight over here, walking along **Holly Farm Lane** with **Reedham Primary School** on the right. At the railway bridge, there are good views of the swing bridge down the line.

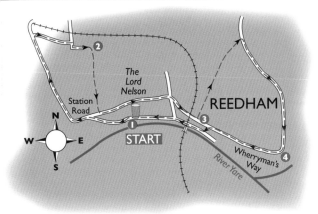

Just after the railway bridge, turn left along a footpath running beside the railway with views over the surrounding marshes. When you reach the lane, turn right, and follow it round to a T-junction.

Turn right onto **Wherryman's Way**. Follow the road uphill for around a quarter of a mile. Turn left down a sloping path, and at the bottom, turn right. Walking parallel to the river and then under a railway bridge, make your way past the **Ship** pub and along **Reedham Quay** back to the **Lord Nelson**.

PLACES OF INTEREST NEARBY

Just a few miles north-east of Reedham village is **Pettitts Animal Adventure Park** (www.pettittsadventurepark.co.uk), home to domestic and exotic animals, rides, live entertainment and a café. A little further afield is **Great Yarmouth**, the 'kiss-me-quick' capital of Norfolk, which has live entertainment on the main pier, a large seafront funfair, the famous Pleasure Beach, and every type of establishment that is synonymous with a large, vibrant seaside town.

Rockland Staithe in the Broads

20 Rockland St Mary

5 miles (8 km)

WALK HIGHLIGHTS

This is a lovely country walk in the southern part of the Broads. These are man-made waterways, comprising around 125 miles of lock-free travel with some amazing wild and natural scenery. It was discovered in the 1950s that the Broads were the result of peat extractions that eventually flooded as the sea levels rose in the fourteenth century. Of all the broads, Rockland is probably the least known but one of the most beautiful. The line of parallel islands north-west of the broad are overgrown hulks of wherries sunk in 1931 to improve water flow. Part of this walk uses the Wherryman's Way, which takes its name from the cargo-carrying sailing barges and the men who worked them at a time when there were no proper roads or railways.

THE PUB

The New Inn, NR14 7HP

☎ 01508 538211 www.thenewinnrockland.co.uk

HOW TO GET THERE AND PARKING: From the A47 Southern Bypass, take the A146 towards Loddon. Turn left almost immediately, and proceed along the Kirby Road through Kirby Bedon and into Rockland St Mary. The pub is situated at the furthest end of the village on the right, opposite the Rockland Staithe mooring area. There are limited car parking spaces at the pub, so you may prefer to use the larger free car park a few hundred metres up the road, which is marked 'Rockland Staithe Car Park'. **Sat nav** NR14 7HP.

MAP: OS Explorer OL40 The Broads. **Grid Ref:** TG 327046.

THE WALK

From the **New Inn** car park, cross the road, and turn right, passing the mooring area. Then turn left along the **Wherryman's Way**. Follow the

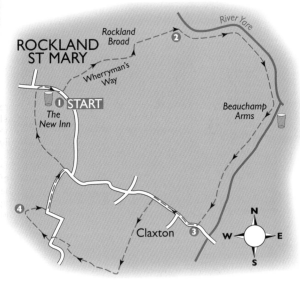

track through a gate. Follow the path; you have the secluded **Rockland Broad** on your left. Pass through the next gate. On your left, you'll notice a bird hide that you might like to visit for some of the best views of the broad. The path veers right, away from the broad and along **Short Dyke** towards the **River Yare**.

2 At the river, follow the riverbank path, with views across **Buckenham Marshes** to your left. Follow the path past a pumping station. Soon you'll come to the **Beauchamp Arms**. Take the footpath to the right as you approach the pub, just before the gate. The path leads away from the river. After a while, you'll come to a gate and then a wider track, which leads onto a tarmac road into **Claxton**.

3 At the T-junction, turn right, passing **Folly Lane** on your left. After a barn conversion on your left, turn left up a track which leads uphill. After half a mile, you'll come to a junction of paths; turn right here. Follow the track downhill to a T-junction. Turn right, and then, after a few metres, turn left through a gap in the hedge, following the path past a house on your left. This path passes through **St Andrew's** churchyard. Exit the churchyard through a gate. Cross the road onto another footpath. Follow this path around the field edge and then as it veers right through the hedge. Cross the next field diagonally towards the trees ahead.

4 Once you are across the field, turn right down the lane. When this track reaches a tarmac road, turn left down the lane, and cross a small stream. Just after the stream, as the road bends round to the right, take the path that goes off to the left. Soon, the track bends sharply right towards a house. At this point, take the path to the left, and walk uphill, following the edge of the field. When you get to a track, turn right. At the main road, turn right, and walk down the hill, returning to the pub.

PLACES OF INTEREST NEARBY
Caistor St Edmund is a village on the River Tas near Norwich and an interesting archaeological site. Artefacts found here narrow down its origins to the first century AD, and it is one of the few Roman towns not to have been damaged or covered up by modern buildings.

Majo

Heart of the Balearics

Jarrold Publishing

CONTENTS

Puerto de Sóller

This is Majorca

Majorca, the largest of the Balearic Islands, has been fulfilling the holidaymaker's dream of sun, sand and sea in an attractive setting for decades. After the Phoenicians, Greeks, Romans, Vandals, Moors and Aragonians had been there the *Illa de la Calma* (Isle of Calm) was finally discovered by the tourists. Since its discovery Majorca has remained 'the' holiday island for an ever-increasing number of holidaymakers. The number of sun-seeking visitors has grown from 70,000 in 1950 to more than four million; the holiday season now lasts all the year round.

Long before our time the earliest inhabitants of Majorca armed themselves with slings. The skilful way in which they used these was necessary for human survival—even the children learned to aim properly. If they hit the meat and fruit which their parents had hung up on a strong bough they were assured of the next meal. How times have changed! Nowadays the delights of Spain's kitchens and cellars are served in the island's restaurants and bodegas. The slings, of course, have found their way into museums, and where watchtowers and forts once circled the island massive holiday resorts have sprung up. The vast majority of tourists spend their holidays in the coastal margins, concentrated in the 1500 or so hotels and apartment blocks which, like castles, protect the more remote beaches and bays, as well as the interior, from further exploitation.

Something for every holidaymaker

Much loved and much maligned, the island has something to offer everybody. Whoever dismisses Majorca as just somewhere the crowds head for does not really know the island. Obviously you do not find peace and quiet in the main resorts. And yet lots of people prefer sunbathing alongside others who also enjoy being

Palma Nova

among the hubbub. During the day they can choose from the well organised variety of sports above and below the water, from horse riding, tennis, golf or volleyball, and at night they can relax in the abundant selection of clubs and discothèques—an active holiday in contrast to the usual routine. And why not indeed?

There are resorts on all the coasts offering entertainment round the clock, such as Playa de Palma, Magaluf, Ca'n Picafort or Cala Millor, and they have well equipped moorings for boats and facilities for watersport enthusiasts.

Should you simply wish to relax on the beach playing with your children or simply doing nothing, then you will find it just right for you. A closer look at Majorca will reveal sunny spots along its contrasting coastlines that are still quiet enough for a holiday off the beaten track — idyllic oases, for example between Cala Santanyi and S'Illot.

Whether you are interested in every sort of sport, discos, the tranquillity of picturesque cliff landscapes, or all three—Majorca meets all these requirements. You will get to know and appreciate that other Majorca, as it really is, on the excursions to strange coastlines or into the picturesque interior of this beautiful island, with its original villages surrounded by majestic olive trees with gnarled and knotted trunks, some of them hundreds of years old. You can walk along the coasts or choose from mountain walks that vary in difficulty.

Celebrated visitors

A holiday on Majorca can be all this. With each visit you get to know more of the diverse beauty and unique character of this island, which it retains despite being a

Moorish residence, Son Alfabia

destination for millions of holidaymakers. Famous visitors have been coming here for years. Notable artists such as the Catalan painter Joan Miró lived and worked here. In the hamlet of Deiá there are exhibitions of artists currently living on the island. It is interesting to read what the first winter guests had to say about their island refuge, including the composer Frédéric Chopin, who wrote 24 immortal preludes while he was living with the writer George Sand in the Chartreuse (Carthusian monastery) at Valldemosa.

Chopin wrote to his friend, 'A turquoise sky, an azure lake, mountains like emeralds, air like heaven. The whole day sunshine and warmth, everyone in summer attire, all evening the sound of guitars and song—in short, a magnificent life.'

In her memoirs George Sand recorded, 'The village of Valldemosa, which is proud of its charter dating back to its Arab origins, nestles in the mountains at the same height as the Chartreuse and looking like its appendage. Almost inaccessible it clings to the mountain like a colony of sandmartins' nests.'

Talking of spending the winter here—the Majorcans invented long-stay holidays. Hotels and tour companies have long specialised in regular winter visitors who want to spend a few weeks or months of the cold season in Majorca's mild climate. Between November and March thousands of shivering Northern Europeans fly to the Balearic Islands. That is only a fraction of the summer figure but sufficient to keep Majorca open all year round. With average temperatures between 15° and 18° C the island provides a pleasant alternative to the fog, frost and snow of our latitudes. The lively island metropolis offers all kinds of distractions, while the tour

Terraced agriculture at Valldemosa

companies and hotels have organised a colourful mixture of entertainment and leisure activities, specially for the winter season.

By the way, spring comes twice to Majorca. In February the white blossoms of the almond trees appear and in April the apple and pear trees are in flower, a delightful invitation to a beautiful holiday resort.

Facts and figures about the island

Majorca, Minorca, Ibiza and Formentera make up the main islands of the Balearic archipelago, which also includes the satellites Cabrera and Dragonera.

Geologically Minorca, formed from chalk and sandstone, is the oldest island of this group. Ibiza is the closest to the mainland, being barely a hundred kilometres from the Gulf of Valencia. The islands are a continuation of the Andalusian mountain fold with the exception of Minorca, which is thought to be a continuation of the Iberian range and therefore the remains of a land bridge between Sardinia and Catalonia.

The Balearics are a Spanish province with the capital Palma de Mallorca (Pop. 316,000). The archipelago is inhabited by a total of approximately 700,000 people. By far the largest proportion live on Majorca (528,000). From its size and geography Majorca, with an area of 3640 sq. km, is the centre of the island group. Minorca (Pop. 62,000), the second largest, has a surface area of 670 sq. km. 71,000 people live on Ibiza (575 sq. km) and Formentera with an area of 100 sq. km has 4700 inhabitants.

On Majorca the main occupation, apart from tourism, is agriculture. The wines of Binisalem and Felanitx and the olive oil from Sóller and Buñola are well known. Other sources of income are the manufacture of shoes, leather goods and furniture, and the production of embroidery and artificial pearls. Tourism, however provides a living for about seventy per cent of Majorca's population.

◆ Phases of History

Prehistoric period (1200 B.C.)

Evidence of the ancient history of the Balearics and their earliest inhabitants is thought to date from the Bronze Age. So-called *talayots, navetas* and *taulas,* presumed to be defence towers, communal tombs and sacrificial altars—architectural clues from ancient times—are to be found particularly on Minorca. There are only a few interesting relics of the Megalithic period on Majorca. The chief ones are the prehistoric remains of the settlement of *Capicorp Vey,* lying on a remote part of the coast south of Lluchmayor, and the *Talayot de Ses Paisses,* on the southern edge of Artá, which is easily accessible. The crudely built prehistoric stone walls have provided welcome building material throughout history. This stone was even used in the foundations of Palma Cathedral.

The first conquerors (800 B.C.)

Slings were the most important weapons of the earliest settlers on the Balearic Islands. They excelled in this form of warfare. Their fame spread throughout the Mediterranean. The name Balearic might have been derived from the Greek word *ballein* (to dart, move quickly). The Phoenicians and Greeks were certainly able to handle this weapon but marvelled at the skills of the first islanders of Majorca, who went about their work naked. The Greeks used to call the island *Gymnesies* – the island of nudes.

The Carthaginians used Ibiza as a base for their military expeditions across the Mediterranean. The 'sling-throwers' were required to provide reinforcements. When the Roman consul Quintus Cecilius Metellus in 123 B.C. executed the decisive blow which led to the conquest of Majorca, the attacking ships were covered with leather hides as protection against the stone missiles of the Majorcans. The Balearics became a Roman colony and *Palmara* (Palma) and *Pollentia* (Alcudia) were founded. For just under half a millennium agriculture and trade expanded. Then the Vandals made a short but bloody appearance. In A.D. 534 the Emperor Justinian attacked the island and conquered it in the name of Byzantium.

The Moors (A.D. 902)

The destruction wrought by the Vandals was followed by a long period of reconstruction. With the arrival of the Moors, A.D. 902, a further peaceful era began. Architects and landowners created new designs. Magnificent oriental palaces, such as the Almudaina in Palma, and splendid mosques were built. A modern irrigation network advanced the agricultural economy. Centuries of Moorish domination left their mark on the islands. The Moorish influence can still be seen today in the names of villages, aspects of folk art and in the language. Yet the Moors were also accomplished pirates. They cold-bloodedly sank ships from the Christian trading fleet in the Mediterranean. In 1174 Berenguer III, Count of Barcelona, failed in his attempt to penetrate the Moorish defences of *Medina Mayurca* (Palma) with the object of putting an end to the piracy.

The Kingdom of Majorca (1229–1349)

In 1229 Jaime I, the king of Aragón (to which Valencia and Catalonia also belonged)—he was twenty and on the threshold of manhood—set sail for Majorca at the head of a Catalonian fleet of 150 ships. His force consisted of 16,000 men,

1500 horses and chariots. The Moors, however, were also prepared for battle; an army of 18,000 warriors and 1000 horses was ready on Majorca. On September 12th Jaime I landed on the south-west coast near Santa Ponsa. In heavy fighting the king of Aragón's army penetrated the fortifications of Palma. At Secar el Real, 5 km to the north, the attack on Palma was prepared. On the final day of 1229 the town's defences gave way—the Christian conquest of Majorca had succeeded. Palma Cathedral is a monument to this historic turning point.

A period of democratic freedom began, bringing to the island and its immigrants from Aragón and Catalonia an independent administration and jurisdiction with guaranteed rights to personal property.

Ibiza also had various masters in the course of history. Like Majorca the former colony of the Phoenicians and Carthaginians (significant exhibits are on display in the archaeological museum of Ibiza town) was ruled in turn by the Romans, Vandals and Byzantines and finally came, in 707, under Arab rule. Jaime I put an end to these changes of ownership with the help of his fleet of 'Conquistadors'. In 1235 the Arab *Yebisah* (Ibiza) succumbed to the Crown of Aragón.

After his father's death in 1276 Jaime II succeeded to the throne and proclaimed the Kingdom of Majorca. Under his regency Palma Cathedral, the new royal Almudaina Palace, Bellver Castle and Valldemosa Castle (on the site of the present-day Chartreuse) were built. He became the mentor of the great philosopher, writer and linguist Ramón Llull, the founder of the first mission school for oriental languages in Miramar (half-way between Valldemosa and Deiá).

In 1287 Minorca was granted to the Kingdom of Majorca. Sancho took over his father's throne in 1311. With his death in 1324 the downfall of the Kingdom of Majorca began. Sancho had no direct successor so his nephew Jaime III, a nine-year-old child, was crowned. A royal council was formed, and the *Consulado de Mar* (Maritime Court) was founded.

But trade and peace were only short-lived. Pedro IV of Aragón was a dangerous rival to the young king who was besieged by the Aragonian troops at Lluchmayor on October 25th 1349. Jaime III fell in open battle and the cruel victor made Bellver Castle into a prison for the widow and children of his brave opponent.

Traditional windmills, found throughout these islands.

King's Palace, Menvan, Palma

Ascendancy of Aragón (14th–15th c.)

The defeat of King Jaime III was the end of the Kingdom of Majorca. The island lost its independence to the royal house of Aragón. In the 14th and 15th c. Palma developed into an important centre of maritime trade (Majorcan cartographers provided the Mediterranean with the most beautiful and accurate maps in the world). The marriage of Ferdinand of Aragón and Isabella of Castile may have finally brought national unity to Spain but the islands were being attacked by the Turks. The population was decimated in the bloody slaughter.

The Turkish admiral Khaireddin Barbarossa was the ringleader of the marauding pirates. Watchtowers and defence posts *(atalayas)* sprang up around the coastline to defend Majorca. Fearing attacks by the Turkish pirates, the population moved away from the coast and built new settlements a few kilometres inland. This accounted for Pollensa developing near the older Puerto Pollensa and Alcudia near Puerto de Alcudia. The castle and town walls of Ibiza are also reminders of those uneasy times.

1701—1839

Majorca's involvement in the War of Spanish Succession (1701–1713) led to further disputes. Majorca and Ibiza declared their support for the Austrian side. The British General Aspheld, who was serving under Spanish command, was sent to Palma to put down the uprising and retake Majorca for the Spanish Crown.

Minorca was constantly in different rulers' hands. In the War of Spanish Succession the British made Mahón, with its large natural harbour, into a naval base. In 1756 during the Seven Years' War this secure port was held by France. The Treaty of Paris returned Mahón to the British, but the year 1782 saw it back in Spanish hands. From 1783 to 1802 the island and harbour were again held by the British.

These are all phases of a changing history. At the end of the Carlist wars (1833–1839) the Balearic Islands finally became subject to the Spanish Crown.

Four distinctive islands

Magaluf, Majorca

Majorca

This pinnacle of tourism definitely has the most to offer in the way of entertainment, nightlife and eating out, as well as a wide choice of sports and activities. A good 80% of visitors to the Balearics come to Majorca. It is not surprising that in the high season the huge beach at Playa de Palma/ El Arenal is not the only one bursting at the seams.

Ibiza

Ibiza is second favourite with the tourists. The 'Isla Blanca' was for a long time an oasis for individuals who liked to explore on their own rather than have the convenience of organised comfort. However, every visitor needs to sleep somewhere, so the number of hotels increased as the airport became busier. Nowadays most of the island's former idyllic sandy bays are surrounded by hotel complexes. Ibiza also offers a wide variety of entertainment, sport, sightseeing and shopping, especially in Ibiza town.

Calaleña beach, Ibiza

View from the Club Náutico, Ibiza

House in local style, El Grao, Minorca

Villa Carlos harbour, Minorca

Minorca

The second largest and least ostentatious of the Balearics has, in relation to its size, fewer hotels than Formentera, although it is true that some concrete towers have been built here. The island is not quite as well provided with sandy beaches as the others. Fjord-like bays are characteristic of Minorca.

Organised entertainment on offer here is more restrained than on Majorca or Ibiza. The local people can still afford to be more relaxed about tourism than elsewhere in the islands, but they are not as self-sufficient as in earlier prosperous times. Dairy produce, fishing, jewellery and leather industries still provide a living but exports are decreasing.

Formentera

Years ago Formentera used to be the secret haven of those seeking solitude away from the crowds, but it has since become much more popular. The visitor who seeks sand, sea and sunshine (and not much else) will find it all here. Hired bicycles, mopeds and cars are the normal means of transport on this picturesque pocket-size paradise. Nightlife is provided by a few discothèques.

Quiet street in Formentera

✖ Food and Drink

Food ranges from simple national dishes to the chef's special

Excursions to the capital Palma, through the countryside or to the villages and fishing ports around the coast can also be journeys through the realm of Majorcan cuisine. During such trips one should sometimes be adventurous. At the tables of a *fonda, posada, hostería* or *bar,* as the unpretentious local cafés are called, you get to know at first hand all about the eating habits and characteristics of the islanders. A glass or two can only help the friendship. Do not be put off by the exterior of the country inns or the carefully patched (plastic) tablecloth.

Sopas mallorquinas, one of the best known specialities, is a stew made from dark wheat bread, assorted vegetables, oil, water and salt. *Tapas*, a colourful selection of titbits consisting of grilled meatballs, mushrooms, fried fish and marinated pieces of vegetables, are eaten at any time of the day. *Sofrit pages* is roast lamb, pork or chicken with fresh vegetables. *Capó a lo Rei en Jaume* is chicken or turkey stuffed with marzipan. *Greixera* is a dish made from meat, eggs, artichokes, peas and broad beans spiced with aromatic herbs. *Caldera de pescado* is a soup made from various kinds of fish with or without rice. *Ensaimada*, a typical pastry, is often filled with pumpkin jam, marzipan or cream. *Pa amb oli*, toast soaked in olive oil and tomatoes, is often eaten with smoked ham—then it is called *Pa amb oli amb cuixot* – a tasty tongue-twister.

Here are recipes for two typical but simple Majorcan dishes to whet your appetite.

Sopas mallorquinas (Majorcan vegetable stew)

The ingredients are easily obtainable except for one thing—you probably will not have any Majorcan bread. It is quite dark when it comes out of the oven, contains no salt and is, of course, made from wheat grown on the island. Leave the bread for a day or two.

Pour sufficient oil into a saucepan to fry some garlic, some fresh onions, a few tomatoes and a few leeks. When it begins to smell inviting add some shredded white cabbage and some water, allowing it all to simmer gently, adding salt and pepper as required. As soon as the liquid is boiling sprinkle the sliced bread with oil and mix it into the shredded cabbage, using equal proportions of bread and vegetable. Then remove the pan from the heat and put on the lid. The bread begins to rise and soaks up the delicious stock.

This recipe can be adapted for different vegetables such as cauliflower, asparagus or spinach according to the season, so you can make sopas mallorquinas at any time of the year.

This hearty meat dish can also be prepared at home:

Majorcan meat stew

Ingredients: 200 gr. loin of pork, 2 pork slices, 1 medium sized slice of pig's liver, 500 gr. potatoes, a red or green pepper, mushrooms as desired, some garlic cloves, salt, paprika, 2 tbsp olive oil, 15 gr. pork dripping.

Heat the oil and fat in a pan. Peel the potatoes and bring to the boil in another saucepan. While they are boiling dice the meat and liver and season with salt and paprika. Add the diced meat to the pan and then add the peppers and mushrooms which have been finely chopped with the garlic. Let it all brown well and finally put in the diced liver, allowing it to cook through. When the potatoes are soft they can be added leaving them to absorb the flavour of the stew. Is that clear? Then *Que aproveche* – Bon appetit!

✄ Festivals and Events

As well as regional festivals in honour of the local saint there is also a series of colourful events, in which the religious aspect by no means rules out such worldly pleasures as dancing, singing and eating. For the visitor it is often great fun taking part in such a *fiesta*.

Some colourful national costumes

Street parade in Palma

Here is a selection:

February: Carnival on Majorca starts at the most beautiful time of the year when the almond blossom is in flower. It lasts ten days and finishes with a joyful procession at Playa de Palma.

March: The festival of *pá i peix* (bread and fish). Pilgrimage to the chapel of Nuestra Señora de la Consolación. Folk dancing and singing (in San Juan).

Holy Week: Procession on Good Friday with the effigy of *Cristo de la Sangre* (in Palma).

Easter: *Devallement* (Festival of the Descent from the Cross). Solemn procession bearing the effigy of Christ. Hundreds of oil lamps and torches light the way (Pollensa).

May: Festival in honour of *Nuestra Señora de la Victoria*. On the following day the attack by Moorish pirates and their defeat (1561) is re-enacted in memory of this dramatic event (Sóller). *Corpus Christi Procession* in all main towns. The carpets of flowers that are laid out for these processions are well worth seeing.

June: Pilgrimage in honour of *San Marcial*. The pottery market with examples of ceramics of the region such as *siurells*, small clay pipes decorated with naive figures (Marratxi), is worth a visit.

July: Festival of the sailors in honour of *Nuestra Señora del Carmen* in nearly all the ports, with processions of boats, fairs and folk-music events. Festival in honour of the saint *Catalina Thomás* of Valldemosa. A sparkling religious and national folk festival (Valldemosa). It continues the next day in Palma with a mounted procession and the symbolic entry of the saint.

August: Festival in honour of the patron saint *San Juan Bautista* (John the Baptist). Procession of the *demonis* (devils) and *cabezudos* (dancers with gigantic face masks) — accompanied by bagpipes (San Juan).

September: Festival in honour of Saint *Catalina Thomás*. A mounted procession and groups of *faies* (flautists) and *xirimies* (pipers) (Santa Margarita). Wine harvest festival. Folk and literary events (Binisalem).

Sailing at Puerto de Andraitx

🚶 Sports and Games

'Sports and games for everyone': this motto is especially true of Majorca. There are renowned sailing and surfing schools (Puerto de Andraitx, Puerto Pollensa) that have long been established here. Keen sub-aqua enthusiasts will find facilities on picturesque cliff coastlines such as Playa de Canyamel, Illetas, Calas de Mallorca and elsewhere.

In recent years tennis and squash have become more widely available. Experienced coaches (at the tennis and squash centre in Cala Millor) will show beginners to the game how to place a cross-court shot perfectly.

There are several 9- and 18-hole golf courses on Majorca. Other sports on offer at many resorts include waterskiing, surfing, paragliding and horse riding. The hotels and tour companies offer recreational activities in their programmes such as gymnastics, volleyball, variety shows, bridge competitions or even courses in computers and languages, all year round. And if all that is not what you are looking for you will find lots of ideas about things to do in this holiday guide.

𝍈 Walking and Mountaineering

Majorca's geology and countryside make it a paradise for walkers and mountain-lovers. Long stretches of sand and dunes invite long, lonely beach walks. Pretty villages off the beaten track entice you into the forests of the hinterland. The bizarre valley of the mountain torrent Torrente de Pareis, an incomparable feat of nature, is a must for the walker. The chain of majestic mountains, thousands of feet high, offers breathtaking all-round views and provides the experienced climber with all types of conditions. You should always ask the locals for advice before setting out on an unknown, unpredictable venture. Novices should stick to the walking and climbing programmes organised by the tour companies. All excursions return to the hotel in the evening. The daily walking times are between four and six hours. There is no need to be afraid of great differences in height on the paths, which are usually well constructed. Among the most scenic routes are the climb to the Puig Teix (1064 m) and the walk through the picturesque valley Barranco de l'Ofre and beyond through the age-old olive grove to Cala Tuent (see map page 74). Hiking boots, adequate clothing and protection against the sun and rain are necessary equipment.

Golden summer scene

 A Children's paradise

Nearly all of Majorca's sandy beaches slope gently into the sea which makes them a paradise for children. The island's hotels welcome children. Most of them have a children's pool near the swimming pool, as do some of the villa and apartment complexes, and one or two even have their own children's playground.

Magaluf Aquapark

The hotels and holiday companies also put on children's parties and various holiday competitions. The children's clubs, supervised by English-speaking children's couriers, cater for even the youngest holidaymakers. There are some marvellous places to go for the whole family: the numerous caves of stalactites both big and small, the Aquapark at Magaluf, trips to the Safari Park, and the dolphin show at Marineland in Costa d'en Blanes.

🚃 Excursions

The second section of this holiday guide contains routes to the most charming places on this island of contrasts. Cars can be hired through the hotel reception or tour company. A smaller car is best for travelling along the tortuous passes and coastal stretches.

Perhaps you could share a car with others and so reduce the hire charge; by this means you acquire independent transport for a reasonable price.

If you choose to travel under your own steam you can plan on using public transport. Some places can even be reached by train. The network of cheap buses facilitates individual, independent travel. Ibiza and Minorca can be reached by air. Both islands are approximately 30 minutes away from Palma by modern jet. The ferry from Ibiza harbour to Formentera takes about 40 minutes. Hire cars are available on all the islands but it is advisable to book in advance for Formentera.

Of course, the tour companies offer a planned programme of excursions, mainly using the buses arranged by local travel agents. Porto Cristo, the Dragon Caves and the Safari Park are among the suggested sights, as well as trips through the idyllic countryside or to the country market in La Puebla. There is an old-fashioned steam train to Sóller, where the boat to La Calobra and the valley of the mountain torrent Torrente de Pareis is waiting. Other activities on offer include pirate boat trips, barbecues, Majorcan folk music or a visit to the monastery of Valldemosa with lunch in an old manor.

Sóller–Palma train

Traditional lace-making, Valldemosa

🛍️ Shopping

The capital Palma is also the shopping paradise of the island. Here you can find antiques, fashions, jewellery, furs and leather goods to suit all tastes and pockets. There are also opportunities for shopping on the excursions across Majorca. Goods typical of the island can be purchased at some centres of manufacture. Santa Maria and Inca are centres of leather processing. In Manacor you can choose from its world-famous artificial pearls. The larger resorts generally have a wide selection of goods on offer. Naturally the souvenir industry makes its presence felt everywhere. When you walk along the beach promenade from Ca'n Pastilla to El Arenal you are left in no doubt as to what you can buy.

🎀 Nightlife

What do you like to do? As far as nightlife is concerned Majorca can meet all your needs. Nowadays nearly every reasonably sized hotel has a bar and discothèque. A choice selection of nightclubs is to be found in Palma, of course. The tour companies will assist you on organised excursions through the nightlife of the metropolis. But there is champagne and celebration on offer round the clock in the major coastal resorts including Playa de Palma/El Arenal, Magaluf, Paguera, Ca'n Picafort, Cala Millor, Puerto de Alcudia and Cala Ratjada.

Hints for your holiday

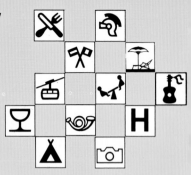

There is no doubt about it—Majorca is a hospitable island which has been specialising for years in catering for tourists from different countries. Evidence of the gastronomic tastes of the British, Germans and Dutch has existed at Playa de Palma, the main holiday resort on the island, for a long time. Several restaurants specialise in the national cooking of these thousands of visitors. There are fish and chips, hot dogs, hamburgers, potato soup with sausages, pork with sauerkraut or Indonesian dishes. Even the most dedicated and tireless lover of fish and seafood gets the occasional craving for steak and kidney pie and a pint of beer. When this happens you can feel almost at home on the long stretch of coastline between Ca'n Pastilla and Arenal (and in the other high-rise resorts).

The island offers infinitely more than just the aroma of familiar food, or the friendly atmosphere of being among compatriots from Liverpool, Newcastle or Cardiff.

Away from the holiday coasts Majorca is still untouched. You should take a look. *Sa Roqueta* (the small rock)—as the locals sometimes call their island—has many fascinating faces. All this makes a holiday on this Balearic island, often superficially dismissed as the destination of the masses, an unforgettable experience.

Immerse yourself in the countryside. During the most beautiful days of the year forget everything back home and enjoy being among your fellow human beings. The Majorcans are also Spaniards and proud of it. To appreciate that, while walking in the picturesque countryside of the island's rural interior, or sitting in the small local cafés that offer unknown delights from the cellar and the kitchen, is to really know what Majorca has to offer. And that amounts to more than Mediterranean sunshine and the gentle temptation of the sea.

Palma — dominated by its cathedral

Where to go and what to see

Palma de Mallorca (Pop. 316,000)

Palma is the capital of Majorca and of the Balearic Islands, a port and trading centre, an episcopal see, an exciting collage of history, commerce and the Mediterranean love of life.

Seeing Palma for the first time from the sea you will be impressed by the wide expansive palm-lined seafront promenade which stretches over six kilometres from the old harbour *Porto Pi* and past the large hotels on the *Paseo Marítimo*, past the modern harbour complex and important architectural monuments to *La Seo* (cathedral). This imposing Gothic building rises proudly above the sea.

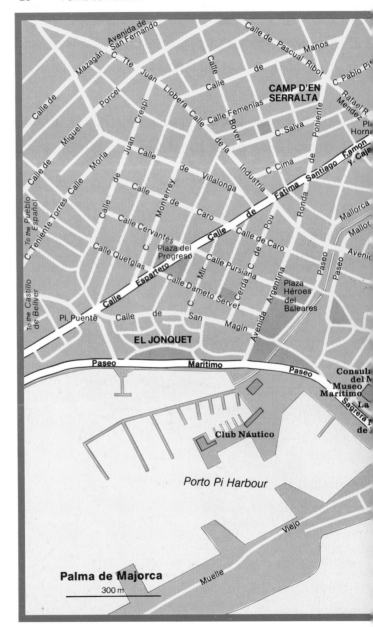

Palma de Majorca

300 m

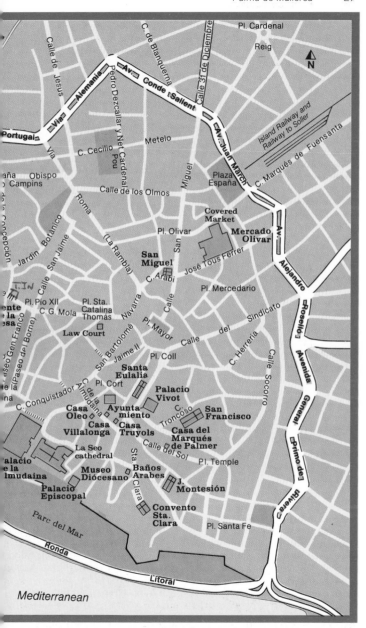

Pl. Cardenal
Reig
N

Calle de Jesús
C. de Blanquerna
Calle 3rd de Diciembre
Via = Alemania
Av. Conde Sallent
Pedro Dezcallar y Net Cardenal Pou
Island Railway and Railway to Soller
Portugal
Via
Metelo
C. Cecilio
Av. Juan March
C. Marqués de Fuensanta
aña Obispo
o Campins
Calle de los Olmos
Miguel
Plaza España
Roma
(La Rambla)
Botánico
Pl. Olivar
Covered Market
Mercado Olivar
Av. Alejandro
Concepción
Jardin
Calle San Jaime
San Miguel
San
José Tous Ferrer
Roselló = Avenida
T. IN
Pl. Pio XII
C.G. Mola
Pl. Sta. Catalina Thomas
C. Arabi
Pl. Mercedario
ente e la esa
Navarra
Pl. Mayor
Calle del Sindicato
General
Pl. Paseo del Borne
Law Court
San Bartolomé
Jaime II
Calle
C. Herreria
Calle Socorro
Primo de
de Gen. Franco
Pl. Coll
e la
ina
C. Conquistador
C. de la Almudaina
Santa Eulalia
Pl. Cort
Palacio Vivot
C. Troncoso
San Francisco
Rivera
Casa Oleo
Ayunta-miento
Casa Truyols
Casa del Marqués de Palmer
Casa Villalonga
La Seo cathedral
Calle del Sol
Pl. Temple
alacio e la lmudaina
Museo Diócesano
Sta. Clara
Baños Arabes
J. Montesión
Palacio Episcopal
Convento Sta. Clara
Pl. Santa Fe
Parc del Mar
Ronda
Litoral
Mediterranean

Palacio de la Almudaina

 Sightseeing

Palacio de la Almudaina

The oldest remains of the town's 2000-year history are to be found here: the foundations of the Palacio de la Almudaina opposite the cathedral date back to the former Roman colony *Palmaria,* which was called *Medina Mayurca* after the Saracen attack in 903. The palace and cathedral are reached from the *S'Hort del Rey* gardens (on Avda. A. Maura) by wide steps that lead up to the *Vila D'Alt* (upper town).

In 1230, following the conquest of the island (see page 8), the seat of the Moorish viziers became the residence of the Majorcan kings. The town was granted its laws and constitution on the authority of Jaime I. Moorish architecture was replaced by Gothic. Even the Almudaina Palace was not spared from the building mania of the various rulers. A door arch and two pinnacle-covered corner towers still betray its Moorish origins. The balcony facing the sea and the chapel of *Santa Ana* (which has a Romanesque doorway) are clearly in Gothic style. Nowadays the Almudaina Palace is used as a summer residence for the Spanish royal family as well as housing the *Capitanía General* (Military Headquarters), the law courts and the city's national museum. The *Patio de Rey,* a beautiful arcaded courtyard and the impressively austere Santa Ana chapel are still easily accessible.

La Seo Cathedral

The cathedral, La Seo, also resulted from one of Jaime I's ideas. According to legend, during a storm on the way to conquer Majorca he pledged to build a church that reached the sky, should victory be his. The central nave of this cathedral, which is regarded as one of the most important examples of Gothic architecture in Spain, measures a proud 44 m in height. The massive sandstone building covers an area of over 6000 sq. m. It is most impressive when seen from the sea.

A mosque used to stand on the square before 1230 when work began on the building, which was to take centuries to complete. The high altar was consecrated in 1346 but the building

Palma Cathedral by day . . .

. . . and by night

Magnificent cathedral door

itself was not completed until 1601. The massive belfry has remained incomplete until the present day. It houses nine bells including the huge *N'Eloi* which has a diameter of two metres and weighs a good 5000 kg. From here one has a panoramic view of the city and harbour. Some alterations were undertaken after the earthquake in 1851, and others during renovations in 1903. The most significant of these was the transfer of the central choir into the *Capilla Real* (Royal Chapel) behind the high altar. Some architectural facts: the Romanesque ground-plan of La Seo is 121 m long and 55 m wide. The ceiling (4000 sq. m) is supported by 14 octagonal pillars each measuring 1.5 m in diameter.

The *main doorway* and the *Puerta del Mirador* are normally closed to visi tors, but you must not miss seeing the latter. Decorating this Gothic doorway are many sculptures and a 'Last Supper' by the important Majorcan architect Sagrera. Entry to the cathedral is from the Plaza de la Almudaina through the *Almudaina Door* under the clock tower when services are being held; otherwise entry is only possible through the museum containing the cathedral treasure (*Tesoro de la Catedral*). Tours take place with commentary in various languages (entry fee). The sharp clear lines of this powerful Gothic church towering up to the sky, with the windows and rosettes of its 30-m-high aisles catching the soft light of a beautiful summer morning, can make this the highlight of your visit. Splendid Baroque altars adorn most of the 18 chapels which surround the mighty cathedral. The tombs of Jaime II and Jaime III are situated on the walls of the *Capilla de la Trinidad* (Chapel of the Holy Trinity) at the end of the chancel. In the two chapter houses exhibits from the cathedral treasure include jewellery, valuable relics, an ivory figure of Christ, chandeliers embossed in silver, a collection of valuable tapestries and even, it is said, splinters from the cross of Christ.

The *Palacio Episcopal* (Bishop's Palace) and *Museo Diócesano* (Diocesan Museum) on the *Bastión del Mirador* are only a few yards away. The *Patio* (inner courtyard) and garden provide a charming sight. A collection of significant Gothic altar paintings and many other exhibits from different centuries of Christian art provides an insight into Majorca's cultural history.

The Old Town

The narrow, pleasantly cool, crooked streets will hold you captive. You will be enchanted by the picturesque patio of the chapel of *San Pedro y San Bernardo*, on the east side of the cathedral, and the façades and courtyards displaying signs of Moorish, Gothic, Renaissance and Baroque influence. These

belong to the houses and palaces of the nobility such as *Casa Oleo, Casa Truyols* and *Casa Villalonga*. They are all located on the Calle de la Almudaina. The charming Renaissance views of the *Casa del Marqués de Palmer* (Calle del Sol, 17) and *Casa del Marqués de Vivot* (Calle Zavella), with a beautiful Baroque staircase and balcony, are close by. The above-mentioned mansions are only a few outstanding examples of the unmistakably Majorcan style of building.

Wandering along the Calle de la Almudaina you also come across the Arab Arch (*Arco de la Almudaina*). This constitutes, together with the Arab baths (*Baños Arabes,* Calle de Serra, 13), the last reminder of Moorish rule. Entry is only permitted to the idyllic gardens of the baths. The *Convento Santa Clara*, which is nearby in Calle Santa Clara, is also reminiscent of the Arab period. The Gothic church has a distinctive clock tower which is similar to a minaret.

Churches and Monasteries

To visit all the churches and monasteries would take several days. Here is a small selection of the most important sacred buildings in Palma.

Coming from the Convento Santa Clara you are already on the way to the *Montesión* church (Calle del Viento). The *Baroque Doorway*(1633) and the Gothic *Marian Altar* (15th c.) by an unknown Majorcan master are worth seeing.

A few streets to the north and you are in the square named after the *Monastery of San Francisco*. The Gothic church has a single nave (74 m long, 17 m wide and 24 m high). The Baroque entrance decorated with a rosette is noteworthy and so is the Gothic tomb inside the church of the great philosopher and father of Majorca's written language Ramón Llull (1232–1315). The peaceful atmosphere of the cloisters with the masterly architecture of the Gothic pointed arches is a haven

for the visitor. The next stop on this tour of Palma's churches is on the same route — the Gothic church of *Santa Eulalia*. Like the cathedral it was begun soon after the conquest, at first as a small chapel (1236), but finishing as a triple-aisled church in 1414. The doorway and clock tower are later additions. Interesting things to see are: the *high altar* with the 'Coronation of the Virgin Mary' by Mezquida, the marble statue 'Dormición de la Virgen' (The Sleeping Virgin), the painting 'Salvator Mundi' (Saviour of the World) by Francisco Gómez, and a Gothic altar painting in the first side chapel on the right.

Heading west you finally reach the *Plaza Cort* with the *Ayuntamiento* (town hall). The impressive 16th c. Renais-

sance façade is particularly interesting. A picture of St Sebastian, the patron saint of Palma (probably by Van Dyck), hangs on the stairway. On the second floor can be seen the *Historical Archives of Majorca* with such valuable manuscripts and documents as the Book of Privileges (*Libre dels privilegis*) of the kings of Majorca.

La Lonja — Paseo Marítimo — Paseo Sagrera

Now the route goes back towards the cathedral and leads down the steps again to the *Vila de Baix* (lower town). The gate to the seafront promenade is called the *Avda. Antonio Maura*. There are numerous restaurants here with tempting menus of seafood, lobsters and prawns, so you can afford to be choosy.

Romantic Palma harbour by night

Left: Palma

By the harbour between the *Muelle Viejo* (Old Pier) and the *Club Náutico* stretches the *Paseo Sagrera*. *La Lonja* (the Exchange), the most important Gothic secular building of the town, is situated here. Built in the 15th c. by the Majorcan architect Guillermo Sagrera, it is an impressive monument to former Mediterranean trading power. You can climb up two of the four octagonal pinnacled corner towers, which provide excellent views across the harbour and town. The richly decorated main doorway crowned with the relief of an angel is impressive. Inside the sandstone building the only decoration consists of six palm-like columns opening up into a cruciform vault. The *Museo Provincial de Bellas Artes* (Provincial Museum of Fine Arts) is now housed here, with Gothic paintings, archaeological items and various exhibitions. The *Consulado del Mar*, the former Maritime court, is situated next to the Museum of Fine Arts. Today this splendid building, with a richly panelled Renaissance balcony consisting of five arches, is the seat of the provincial government. The *Museo Marítimo* (Maritime Museum) containing information about Majorca's seafaring history used to be situated here.

The Paseo Sagrera recalls another chapter of history. Until the 17th c. the turbulent *La Riera*, which used to run along what is today the *Via Roma* (also called La Rambla) and the so-called *Borne* (Paseo Generalísimo Franco), separating the upper and lower towns from each other, entered the sea here. This mountain torrent claimed about 5000 lives in 1403. The 17th c. was also characterised by catastrophes. Drought, hunger and plague spread through the town. The War of Succession between Austria and the Bourbons found Palma on the side of Austria, so when the island was occupied by the troops of Philip V Palma was robbed of all its autonomous privileges, and from then on was a simple island town.

Paseo del Borne—La Rambla

Not all was good that came out of the 19th c. as far as 'La Ciudad' was concerned. Several epidemics, among them yellow fever, decimated the population. However, about this time the wide boulevards were built—the Paseo del Borne and the Promenade La Rambla (Via Roma). Electricity, the new power source of our century, brought an economic and political revival to Palma. In about 80 years the population of the city had more than quadrupled. The *Plaza Mayor* used to be the market place of the town; it was renovated in the early seventies. Nowadays shops, bars and small restaurants dominate the scene. Our route follows the former bed of the mountain torrent La Riera over the *Avenida Antonio Maura* to the well-known promenade Paseo del Borne, popularly known as *Borne*. This wide prestigious boulevard is sprinkled with café terraces, restaurants, travel agencies and high-class shops. The shady plane trees provide a meeting place to chat with friends and watch the visitors from all over the world strolling by.

Take a few steps to the west and you come to one of the two most imposing houses of the nobility, the *Casa Marqués de Sollerich* (Calle San Cayetano 22). The façade, balcony and courtyard of this mansion built in the Italian style are worth seeing. It contains a valuable collection of furniture and paintings of Majorcan origin from the 18th c.

There is another mansion to add to the tour of Palma's grand houses. A few minutes away in a north-easterly direction you arrive at *Casa Berga* (Plaza Santa Catalina Thomás 40). This is the second largest palacio in Palma and nowadays used as a courthouse. Points of interest include the doorway covered in coats-of-arms, the façade decorated with balconies and the large courtyard.

From the Borne the streets lead into the shopping centres. The *Plaza de Pio XII* opens out to the north with the

Typical village clinging to the hillside, north of Palma

bubbling Turtle fountain in the centre (also called *Fuente de la Princesa*). It was built in 1833 in memory of the Infanta Isabella. To the left is the *Avenida Jaime III* with boutiques, banks, travel agencies and airline offices.

At the southern end of the Borne from the *Plaza de la Reina* (with the pretty park *Glorieta de la Reina*) to the Plaza Mayor there are shops catering for every possible demand tucked away in the crooked little narrow streets. A stroll through the *Calle San Miguel* to the north of Plaza Mayor leads to the market halls of Palma in the *Plaza Olivar*. The *Mercado Olivar* offers an inviting selection of meat, fish, fruit, vegetables and tapas amidst the hustle and bustle of Majorcan life.

The *Calle San Miguel*, past the church of the same name, and the *Calle Arabi* finally lead to the majestic Via Roma or La Rambla (jewellery, antiques and flower market). Along *Calle Navarra* (Teatro Principal), *Calle General Mola* and *Plaza de Pio XII* you return to the shady Borne.

The nearby seafront promenade from the *Paseo de Sagrera* to the *Paseo Marítimo*, called after its engineer *Avenida Ingeniero Roca*, with its expensive hotels, restaurants and shops is worth an evening stroll. Across the Paseo Marítimo the entertainment quarter *El Terreno* is vast and the famous windmills of *El Jonquet* have long since been turned into nightclubs with the increased prosperity brought by tourism.

The Paseo Marítimo stops at the old harbour Porto Pi, with the lighthouse and watchtower *Torre de Pelaires* (15th c.).

Pueblo Español

From the seafront esplanade more sights on the outskirts of Palma become visible. The Pueblo Español, which was built at the beginning of the 1960s, is a microcosm of the Spanish landscape: a modern complex consisting of congress halls and theatres, lifelike imitations of Spanish secular and sacred architecture, replicas of Spanish towns and villages, monuments from various periods and regional Spanish folk art. Providing a lively contrast there are examples of contemporary artistic handicrafts (and junk), taverns, restaurants, folk festivals and flamenco shows (in the *Tablao Flamenco*).

Castillo de Bellver

The Castillo de Bellver dominates the western town—to a certain extent it forms an architectural contrast to the cathedral. (Bus service from the Plaza de la Reina.) The castle dates from the beginning of the 14th c. and was at first the summer residence of the kings of Majorca. Surrounded by pines it stands 140 m above the sea with magnificent views. After the battle of Lluchmayor in 1349 in which Jaime III lost his life, the victor Pedro IV of Aragón turned the castle into a prison for King Jaime's relatives. Bellver castle fulfilled this dismal role for some time afterwards. In the 16th c. it was a state prison for political prisoners and eventually also for criminals. The most notable prisoner was the minister and writer Jovellanos. A bust in the park and a plaque in his cell commemorate his imprisonment from 1802 until 1808, which he spent writing some important works. The mighty *Torre del Homenaje* (Tower of Honour) was linked by a bridge to the terrace of the main building. However, the tower had a function which belies its name—it actually served as a dungeon. The darkest of all cells had a hole in the ceiling which was the only connection with the outside world, so it acquired the name *La Olla* (deep pot). Nowadays one can enjoy an uninterrupted view over the bay and town from the Torre del Homenaje. The castle courtyard with its fountains and romantic arcades is also interesting. The *Museo Municipal* (Municipal Museum) contains finds from prehistoric times.

Castillo de Bellver

relaxing here without too much hustle and bustle. If you want a change Palma is not far away.

 Small partly concreted strip of sand in Illetas itself which is equipped as a bathing beach. Several small sandy coves are close by. The family hotel *Bon Sol* has its own beach.

 Pedalos on the seafront.

 Schools.

 In most hotels (heated in winter).

 Several hotels have courts.

 Air pistol and rifle shooting in the Hotel *Bonanza Playa*.

Illetas Bay

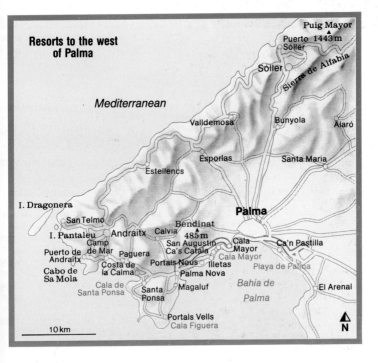

Palma Nova

 Special interest courses and language courses in the Hotel *Bonanza Playa*.

H Sauna, massage and gymnastics in the Hotel *Bonanza Playa*.

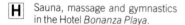 *Pepe's* and *Bonaire* (Spanish cuisine), *ABC* (international cuisine).

♫ *Golf, Napoleon, La Sirena*.

♀ *Pepe's Bar* (Flamenco music); *Kalkutta* (show).

🚌 Bus service Illetas–Cala Mayor–Palma (every 10 minutes).

Portals Nous/Bendinat
Portals Nous also consists of pretty coves. The sand on the little beach is clean and light-coloured. Fishing boats and the older heart of the town provide delightful splashes of colour in this recently much developed holiday centre which extends along the slopes in the shade of pine trees. You can find peace and quiet here in charming surroundings, away from Palma and yet not too far away.

The neighbouring development Bendinat also appears quiet and well maintained with its elegant villas descending in terraces to the cliff coast. There are rocky beaches which have been levelled with concrete and a medium-class hotel with a lovely view.

🏖 Small sandy beach, small coves suitable for swimming not far away.

 In various hotels (heated in winter).

⚲ School. ✓ 9-hole course.

✗ *Tristan* (nouvelle cuisine, rather expensive, German management).

📷 *Castillo de Bendinat* at the base of the hill of the same name (485 m). Picturesquely situated 18th c. castle with a park. Dolphinarium at *Marineland* on the road to Palma Nova (Zona Residencial Costa d'en Blanes). Bus service Palma Nova–Palma (every 15 minutes).

Palma Nova/Magaluf
The twin resorts of Palma Nova/Magaluf lie on the western edge of the expansive *Bahía de Palma* (Bay of Palma). The short stretch of motorway which conveniently links the above resorts south-west of Palma with the island's capital finishes here at the moment.

Magaluf

Palma Nova

Compared with its southern neighbour Magaluf, Palma Nova still seems like a well kept suburb of villas despite the concentration of hotels, bungalows and apartment blocks. The little fishing and yacht harbour even has an old-fashioned, easy-going air about it. The bay curves round against a background of small inviting pine woods. Both narrow beaches at the *Paseo del Mar* are completely packed during summer weekends. Restaurants, cafés and all sorts of shops are to be found on the well tended main beach and promenade.

Magaluf

Magaluf began as a continuation southwards of Palma Nova. The planners embraced tourism here on a massive scale. The high buildings of the giant hotels and apartment blocks tower upwards into the holiday sky like long fingers. During the high season the beautiful golden beach becomes a densely populated oasis for bathers between the concrete and the sea. The broad streets of this resort offer a wide choice of shops and entertainment to suit every taste.

Palma Nova: On the Paseo del Mar there are two sandy beaches with palm trees and pines growing here and there. To the north at the little yacht harbour there is also a small beach, and another, approximately 200 m long, by the hotels in the southern part of the resort; it is well maintained, with golden sand and ample bars, barbecues, pedalos, etc.

Magaluf has a longer beach of light golden sand, about 400 m by 15 m. It is very crowded in the high season and not always as clean as it might be. The gently sloping beach is ideal for children.

In various hotels (heated in winter).

S School. Also scooters.

Tennis club next to the Dolphinarium.

Arranged through hotels and tour companies.

Mesón Son Caliu, Amador, Can Miguel (Spanish cuisine); *Tabu* (international cuisine).

Casino Mallorca in the elegant development of Cala Xada on the scenic steep cliff coast.

Barabas, Borsalino, Kopelius.

Post bus (from Monday to Friday 10 a.m. until 11.30 a.m.).

 Urgencias Médicas, tel. 68 15 18; *Clinic Balear,* tel. 68 14 15; *Salus,* tel. 68 05 83; *Centro Médico,* tel. 28 58 58.

 Bus services Magaluf–Palma Nova–Palma run every 15 minutes. Playasol bus company operates between Palma Nova and Palma every 30 minutes.

Portals Vells

About 9 km to the south. To reach the unspoilt sandy cove of Portals Vells you follow a narrow track through pine woods, past an old passenger plane fitted out as a bar. The track is narrow and you should watch out for pot-holes. The road to the lighthouse on the peninsula of *Cala Figuera* leads past small romantic rocky coves but ends at a restricted military zone.

 Pedalos.

 Small restaurant, beach bar.

 Portals Vells has an extensive and beautifully situated 18-hole golf course, the *Club Golf de Poniente,* open to non-members.

Santa Ponsa

At Santa Ponsa 5 km west of Magaluf tourists are well catered for. A major motor road leads to the wide indentation that is the bay of Santa Ponsa. In the high season the many guests staying in the hotels and apartment blocks flock to the small pretty bay fringed with pines to secure their places in the sun. The resort is popular and offers lots of activity, entertainment and an extensive selection of shops concentrated in a small area. Other attractions include a yacht club and neighbouring golf course.

Old Santa Ponsa also has its place in the island's history. Jaime I landed here in 1229 during the conquest of Majorca. This historical event is commemorated by a stone cross on the edge of the bay.

Between other developments such as *Malgrat* and *Costa de la Calma* (club hotel with vast choice of sport and entertainment) across the steeply rising southern edge of the bay lies the smart villa resort of *Costa de la Luz,* amidst picturesque hilly countryside and surrounded by pines. Even here further development is taking place. The beach is rocky, levelled in places, and there are a few hotels and restaurants.

 A beach of fine sand 300 m long and up to 60 m wide. Suitable for children it is clean and slopes gently to the sea. It has a café-bar, beach huts, showers and sun loungers.

  In various hotels (heated in winter).

 3 km; open to visitors (18 holes).

 In certain hotels.

 For the long-stay winter visitor there are various entertainment, fitness and special interest programmes as well as language courses in the club meetings organised by the major tour companies. Chess and card competitions, variety shows, plays and dances.

 Also through hotel reception and tour companies.

 Victoria (good value, near the beach). *Xaloc, Las Vegas, Park Club, Sa Masia.*

 Caramba, Byblos   Cala Xada.

 Urgencias Médicas, tel. 69 00 47; *Salus* medical centre, tel 68 05 83; *Clinic Balear,* tel. 69 11 11.

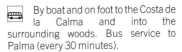 By boat and on foot to the Costa de la Calma and into the surrounding woods. Bus service to Palma (every 30 minutes).

Paguera

There is no motorway between Palma Nova and Paguera but the coast road is very well constructed here – unfortunately it runs through the centre of Paguera. In spite of this, the well kept, beautiful wide beach makes the resort into a pleasant place to stay. An attractive contrast to all the concrete here is provided by the hilly hinterland with its olive groves and woods; this is the start of the spectacular mountain range of the west coast. The main thoroughfare of Paguera has everything a holidaymaker could want – all sorts of shops, cafés, bars and boutiques. You can easily find restaurants which have British 'home cooking' on the menu. In addition there is a varied choice of discos and nightclubs for the early hours.

 One of the best beaches of the south-west coast. The main beach extends for about 250 m. To the right of Hotel *Lido Park* there is a somewhat smaller sandy beach edged by pinewoods, gently sloping and ideal for children. Other smaller concreted bathing areas.

🛶 🛶 In various hotels (heated in winter).

🏄 On the rocky coast. School.

🏄 School.

🔲

🔺 Pedalos.

🎾 Several hotel courts.

Ｕ School.

 Also through hotel reception and tour companies.

 Also scooters.

 El Cordobés (tapas, international cuisine); *La Dragonera* (Majorcan cuisine); *Mesón de Paguera* (fish specialities); *La Pampa, Cupidor* (international cuisine); *Los Cazadores* (fish and Spanish cuisine); *Casa Rústica* (German cuisine).

🎵 *Graf Zeppelin, Mississippi, Pygmalion, Alexandra.*

Paguera

Cala Xada.

 Urgencias Médicas, tel. 68 64 09; *Clinic Balear*, tel. 68 66 66; *Salus*, tel. 68 62 34; *Centro Médico*, tel. 68 71 76.

 Along the coast and into the surrounding woodlands. Regular bus service to Palma (weekdays hourly, public holidays mostly hourly).

Cala Fornells
This pretty cove situated about 1 km south of Paguera is densely populated but the hotels, villas and apartments have been built in an attractive neo-Moorish style. There are paved bathing terraces on the small sandy beach.

  In the hotels.

Camp de Mar
This small holiday village just 4 km west of Paguera is a haven for those who seek unspoilt beach life. The small picturesque sandy cove overlooks an island which is accessible by a narrow bridge near some paved areas. It is not at all pretentious here. There are also a few hotels.

 The small bay has a sandy beach, about 100 m by 50 m, from which you can swim. It slopes gradually to the sea and is ideal for children. There are a few beach huts, sun loungers, parasols and a beach bar.

 Pedalos.

 In two hotels.

Puerto de Andraitx
A pleasant winding road leads to the sailing enthusiast's paradise – Puerto de Andraitx. Fishing boats and sumptuous yachts are moored alongside each other in this natural harbour lying at the foot of the steep slopes of *Cabo de Sa Mola*. There is a modern marina in front of the fishing harbour on the opposite side of the bay. Exclusive complexes of holiday villas are grouped on the slopes of the hinterland. You will search in vain for sandy beaches here. The houses by the harbour front have paved patios and mooring berths instead. The sailors here sail close to the wind and are busy at the helm during the day, so they don't really mind the lack of discos in the evenings.

 El Celler; *Roccamar* (fish); *El Coche* (Spanish); *Foc y Fum* (international, on the road to Andraitx town).

 Bus service to Palma 3 times daily.

 School.

San Telmo
The drive to Majorca's most westerly resort over winding hilly roads is certainly taxing, but full of variety. San Telmo is still one of the most unspoilt spots for swimming in the extreme south-west of Majorca. Expensive villas and apartments are, however, being built even here. The centre of the quaint fishing village is still intact.

Two rugged rocky islands *Pantaleu* and *Dragonera* lie off the coast of this deep-set bay with its small dark-coloured sandy beach. In the foreground of this impressive coastline there are numerous little patches of sand and rock. The background consists of pinewoods and forbidding hills.

 Small sandy beach, suitable for children. Showers.

 Punt Blanc, Dragonera, Flexas (all are Spanish restaurants).

Local fisherman mending his nets

To the islands off shore and their fascinating diving grounds; into the wooded surrounding countryside, and also a 2-hour walk to the former Trappist monastery *Sa Trappa*. Bus service to Palma (via Andraitx, several times a day).

Puerto de Sóller (Pop. 1000)

The town and harbour of Sóller are situated on the north-west coast, in the rugged domain of the *Costa Brava Mallorquina* – Majorca's 'wild coast'. Puerto de Sóller has one feature which distinguishes it from all other resorts: the nearby town of Sóller has a direct railway line to Palma. A wonderful old engine from the Siemens-Schuckert works steams along the 35-km track at the breathtaking speed of about 50 km per hour; the journey takes an hour. It is an interesting trip through fruit and olive plantations and through 14 splendid tunnels, the longest penetrating the *Sierra de Alfabia*. For the harbour you get out and board an airy open narrow-gauge tram with a warning bell.

The wide, sheltered curve of the once important commercial harbour can accommodate even quite large vessels. The local fishermen's catch is served up in the restaurants at Puerto – delicious and freshly cooked. The resort extends along the bottom of the bizarre slopes of the *Sierra de Torellas* where the highest mountain on the island *Puig Mayor* (1443 m) is to be found.

The seafront promenade is bustling with activity during the day. The harbour's commercial traffic and pleasure boats, together with the numerous day trippers' coaches, make for that vibrant atmosphere which is cherished by the many visitors and sightseers. The resort also has a corresponding quota of boutiques, souvenir shops, restaurants and bars of every type. In the evenings it calms down and becomes quite peaceful.

The two beaches, however, are nothing special. The small medieval town of Sóller (see page 76), 5 km from Puerto de Sóller, is charming with its

Mountain village of Deiá

narrow little streets and its friendly plaza inviting you to stop and have a drink, to see what is going on and to be seen.

🏖️ The more attractive of the two beaches is on the edge of the extensive harbour basin. It is narrow and not particularly well kept. The other bathing area is not far from the harbour. It is very pebbly and has beach huts and showers.

🛌 In numerous hotels (heated in winter).

🏊 School.

🎠 🎿 For long-stay winter visitors there are various entertainment and special interest programmes as well as language courses in the club meetings organised by the major tour companies. Chess and card competitions, variety shows, theatre and dance evenings, library, etc.

🍴 *Atalya Club* (international, expensive prices); *Es Canys* (international); fish restaurants around the harbour; French cuisine along the seafront.

🚌 Boat trips along the Costa Brava, excursions into the Sierra. Railway excursion to Palma.

Puerto de Sóller

Puerto Pollensa

The North Coast

Puerto Pollensa (Pop. 300)

Visitors to the island who wish to spend a little longer getting to know the exceptional beauty of Majorca's north coast head for the sweeping bay of Pollensa. Puerto Pollensa is still an unspoilt fishing harbour and is near the provincial town of Pollensa (see page 82), 6 km away. The hotels and developments on the harbour's edge, mostly of medium standard, have until now been the only evidence of the advance of tourism. Life centres around the harbour pier. There are friendly restaurants and street cafés, where fishermen and visitors rub shoulders.

The main beach, which is gently sloping, consists of golden sand and is backed by pines. Fishing boats are to be found here. The sands stretch for several kilometres, as far as Alcudia, but soon become unattractive. To the north of the harbour there is another narrow sandy beach.

Cala Pi: golden sandy beach (about 250 m in length and dotted with pines) in front of the luxury *Formentor* hotel. From the boat jetty there are trips to have coffee at the island's best-known hotel. Part of the hotel beach is reserved for guests. The public beach is not in very good condition.

   At many hotels.

   School.

  Club Náutico.

Cala de San Vicente

The unspoilt and idyllic resort of Cala de San Vicente lies hidden about 6 km to the north of the small country town of Pollensa. A few medium-sized hotels, holiday villas and restaurants have been built near the small golden sandy beach. Three other small coves complete the picture. There is an impressive view of *Cabo Formentor* (see page 83). There are excellent opportunities for diving here, against a background of karst cliffs, pine trees and olive groves; all this is part of the individual and peaceful character of the resort. To spend the whole of your time here is to leave behind modern holiday activity in exchange for the simple tranquillity of island life.

 Four small coves with golden sand, basically equipped.

 Various hotel courts.

 At various hotels.

Puerto de Alcudia (Pop. 500)

The once fortified town of Alcudia lies 1.5 km from its harbour. Puerto de Alcudia nestles in the broad crescent of the bay of the same name. The north-west flank of the bay is formed by a bizarre peninsula leading to the *Cabo del Pinar*; the eastern arm leads to the *Cabo Ferrutx*. The attraction of Puerto de Alcudia is its beautiful expansive, pine-fringed sandy beach. Unfortunately the unimaginative architecture of this holiday resort does little to relieve the monotonous character of the coastal landscape. Behind the holiday façade

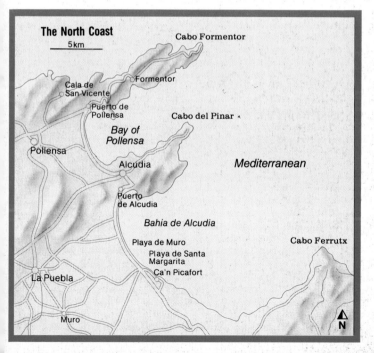

The road climbs towards Cabo Formentor

development is far from finished. However, the short seafront promenade has numerous cafés where you can meet and chat. Puerto de Alcudia is ideal for families and if you want to enjoy sun and sand there are plenty of facilities for water-sports.

Extensive well maintained beach of white sand with beach huts, showers, sun loungers, parasols, etc. It is well equipped and slopes gently, so it is perfect for children. An almost 11-km-long white sandy beach stretches towards *Ca'n Picafort* past various developments.

In numerous hotels.

S School at the hotel *Sunwing*. It is possible to enter for the A-certificate.

School.

Pedalos.

Various hotel courts (with coaching).

U School.

Also through hotels and tour companies.

Bogavante, *Loro Verde* (Spanish and international cuisine); *Lovento* (fish restaurant); *Venezia* (international cuisine); *La Pizzeria* (Italian menu).

Menta (with swimming pool), *Bloc's, Bellevues, Calypso, Bell's.*

Ferry connection to Minorca, boat trips to Puerto Pollensa and to Cabo Formentor. Regular bus services to Alcudia, Pollensa, Ca'n Picafort (hourly) and Palma (several times a day).

Alcudia town (daily 9 a.m.–1 p.m.).

 The main beach *Playa de Santa Margarita*, gently sloping and ideal for children, is well equipped but not always clean. To the west it turns into dunes. To the east there is a second, medium-sized sandy beach, *Son Baulo*, broken by rocks. It is in an attractive setting backed by pine woods, clean and with a bar, sun loungers and parasols. Further west *Playa de Muro* is an elegant, prettily located holiday complex with unspoilt sand dunes.

In various hotels (heated in winter).

School.

Pedalos.

School.

Various hotel courts and *Club Rojo Vivo*.

For long-stay winter holidaymakers there are numerous entertainment and special interest programmes, as well as language courses, held in the clubs run by the major tour companies.

Also through hotels and tour companies.

Mandlego (fish specialities); *Club Náutico, Bodega Florit, Can Toneu, Caty* (Majorcan dishes); *La Bota, Las Farolas* (Spanish and international cuisine); *Frankfurt* (German cuisine).

Skau, Charly's, Clumba, Tiffany's, Cran Filou, Rojo (in Son Baulo).

Regular bus service to Alcudia, Pollensa and Palma.

Post van weekdays in front of Hotel Galatxia (1 and 4 p.m.).

Urgencias Médicas, tel. 52 74 11, night 52 73 70.

 Urgencias Médicas, tel. 54 55 24.

Ca'n Picafort (Pop. 800)

The wide beach of the old fishing harbour has turned the village into a tourist resort. The beach stretches over 11 km to Puerto de Alcudia and consists of real 'seaside' sand. Unfortunately there has been a great deal of development here, starting at the very entrance to the resort amongst the pine trees. The old harbour on the right-hand side provides a pleasant contrast to the concrete silhouette which uncompromisingly follows the coastline for miles. Narrow streets lead to the seafront promenade between high-rise hotels and the close network of bars, shops and amusement arcades. Efforts are being made to smarten up the buildings and make their surroundings more attractive, but new development is still taking place relentlessly.

Majorca's only official camp site lies on the northern edge of the town.

Fabulous bathing beaches

The South Coast

Cala Blava/Cala Pi/La Rápita

Should you wish to escape from the bustling beach at El Arenal (see page 40) in the high season for a day or so, you can head for some smaller beaches in the south, both sandy and rocky. They can be reached by minor coast roads.

Just 3 km away you come to the neat holiday villas of Cala Blava where the rocky landscape is easily accessible. The next developments en route to Cala Pi are architecturally superior and the hotels are more exclusive. The steep coast here is quite accessible for swimming. A small detour through the flat interior finally brings you out at the holiday resort of Cala Pi (about 30 km from El Arenal) which is growing up along the beautiful cliff coast. The plots of land marked out in the wooded countryside show that there are still plans to develop tourism further in this area which was once the refuge of pirates; it is a picturesque and quiet place to stay but without a sandy beach, ideal however for underwater-sports enthusiasts.

The road leads back inland for about 12 km and via the unspoilt little fishing port of S'Estanyol, with more basic holiday accommodation, to the neighbouring rustic development of La Rápita on the flat rocky coastline. At the small yacht harbour there is a *Club Náutico.*

Heading south-east you may be surprised to come to an inviting 2.5-km beach of white sand dunes which slopes gently and is in a very attractive setting. It stretches as far as the unpretentious resort of *Ses Covetes* close by.

Colonia de Sant Jordi (Pop. 400)

An aspiring holiday village is growing south of *Campos del Puerto* about 12 km from the main Palma-Santanyi road. It is situated near the little fishing village of *Puerto de Campos* on a wide sweeping sandy bay fringed by pine trees and with the natural protection of rock formations. Above the flat rocky coast several sizeable hotels and numerous guest houses together form a nucleus of tourist accommodation, around which holiday villas and apartments are appearing in great numbers. This friendly rural holiday resort has lots to offer water-sports enthusiasts. Further inland where it is quite flat there are salt works and agricultural land under cultivation.

 Well maintained main beach in a wide bay. A jetty separates it from another sandy beach interspersed with rocks. A 2.5-km unspoilt sandy beach with dunes to the west near *Ses Covetes*.

 In numerous hotels (also a seawater pool).

 Children's playgrounds in several hotels.

  Schools.

At the water-sports centre on the main beach.

 Pedalos.

 Numerous hotel courts.

 Rancho Andrés.

Also through hotel reception and tour companies.

 Also covered pedal-cars.

 Mar y Sol, Casa Pepe and *Antonia* (Spanish, fish, paella); *El Puerto* (international cuisine).

 Los Pinos, Sant Jordi.

Dr Miguel Vicenz, tel. 65 54 58 and 64 92 74.

Excursions to Palma and Santanyi with its beaches. Regular bus service between Ses Salines and Palma (about 3 times daily).

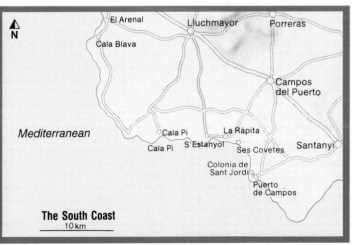

The South Coast
10 km

Cala Santanyí

The East Coast

Cala Figuera/Cala Santanyi

The main road C-717 from Palma ends after about 50 km in the little country town of *Santanyi*. After finding your way around its narrow back streets and then out along the wide approach road you will discover two charming places on the south-eastern coast. The first is Cala Figuera, a small picturesque fishing port hidden on the south-east coast in a deeply incised bay resembling a fjord. There are a few natural caves and some quite formidable rocks which shelter the harbour from the sea. The seafront promenade makes a delightful subject for your camera. A handful of bars and restaurants sometimes have seats outside. In view of the steep rocks you need to be quite agile before you can jump into the water. The fishermen are still content with their simple cottages but, in contrast, the new settlers have built rather more grandly.

 In two hotels.

  Hotel courts.

 Cala Marina and *San Pedro* (Spanish), *Pizzeria*.

 Mondbar, La Trompa, 'J', E. Castillo, roller-skating disco.

Bus service to Palma (in the high season from Cala Figuera, in the low season from Cala Santanyi — 3 times a day).

Pretty Cala Santanyi does not have any fishing boats but it does have a lovely sandy beach on a fjord-like inlet backed by steep cliffs and pine woods. Peace and quiet still exist here. Up to now the hotels on the Playa and on the cliffs have not had a significant effect on this idyllic place. A more extensive villa complex lies on the cliff top opposite; access to the bay is by a steep path.

A clean, gently sloping beach, about 150 m by 100 m, with sun loungers, parasols, etc.

Pedalos.

Bus service Santanyi — Palma (several times a day).

Strawberry pickers

Porto Petro/Cala Mondragó

In the wide harbour bay of Porto Petro fishing boats and leisure craft bob up and down harmoniously alongside each other. Yachtsmen and lovers of delicious fish specialities meet here. The harbour restaurants are simple but this does not detract from the quality. You can swim in the surrounding bays.

Porto Petro is also the gateway to Cala Mondragó. The narrow approach road has been tarmacked for the visitors. A bumpy road also leads from Santanyi through gorgeous woodland and moorland, but ends abruptly with a view across the bay. The rest of the way is a ten-minute walk which is not all that easy. Cala Mondragó enjoys a delightful position away from all the activity. Two attractive white sandy beaches lie on the opposite sides of a wide inlet. They are connected by a paved cliff path. The woods and bushes here have been left to grow wild. Two unpretentious hotels, a few villas and numerous apartments have not spoilt the landscape. This is an ideal location for individuals who want to get away from the crowds.

Two white sandy bays up to 80 m wide. The further one is more sheltered from the current and so more popular.

On the beach there is a simple restaurant and a kiosk.

Cala d'Or/Cala Serena/Marina de Cala d'Or

Cala d'Or

5 km to the north of Porto Petro the magnificent coastline has been developed for tourism. The unusual thing about it is that it has been done with due regard for the scenery. Certainly there are many hotels, pensions and villas jostling to attract as many visitors as possible. Yet the architecture, often in neo-Moorish style, is more tasteful and shows more individuality than in other resorts of comparable size. This development is quite spacious with pleasant shade provided by the numerous pine trees. Gleaming white elegant villas and houses overlook the sea from the rocky strip. The shopping and entertainment facilities are also 'up market'. Bays resembling fjords serve as bathing areas. The sandy beaches are rather on the small side but to compensate are quiet and sleepy. Here and there you can see concrete bathing platforms in the middle of a lovely panoramic cliff coastline.

Cala Gran, Playa d'Or in the resort, *Cala Esmeralda*, 1 km further on. Very clean, sheltered white sandy beaches, gently sloping, well equipped with beach huts, sun

Santueri Castle, near Porto Colóm

loungers, parasols, etc. South of Cala d'Or at the new villa complex of *Cala Egos*, an attractive tiny sandy bay in the cliffs. Just to the north, the scenically curving cliffs of *Cala Ferrera* cove, with hotels and bungalows.

 Schools at the neighbouring cove of *Cala Llonga*.

 Instruction at *Cala Gran* near five reefs.

 Public courts at *Club Hípico*; hotel courts.

 Club Hípico.

 Also scooters and mopeds.

Cala d'Or harbour

 Also through hotel reception and tour companies.

 Sa Torre (Spanish and Majorcan cuisine); *La Cala, Yate d'Or* (fish dishes); *Can Trompe* (Majorcan cuisine); *Don Leone, Copa d'Or* (pizzerias).

 Alfa, Fahrah's.

 Pepe's Bar, Crecendo Bar.

 Post Office at Cala Llonga, open weekdays from 9 a.m. until 2 p.m.

 Salus, tel. 65 31 21; Dr Obrador Vidal, tel. 65 32 25, 65 77 77 (in Santanyi).

 Bus service Cala d'Or–Palma (several times a day).

Cala Serena

About 2 km north of Cala d'Or on a beautiful little sandy bay there is one of the *Robinson Clubs*. This site, set among bougainvillaea and hibiscus, has everything necessary for a sociable sports holiday.

 Sheltered, gently sloping sandy beach.

 Large swimming pool with sun terrace and children's pool.

Children's Club.

 Subaqua.   School.

 11 hard courts, 3 practice areas, 2 indoor courts.

 S'Horta (about 7 km), 9 holes.

 Gymnastics, yoga, sauna.

 Batik, pottery, silk screen printing, etc.

   Boutique.

 Dances, happenings, folk displays, etc., daily.

Marina de Cala d'Or.

At the rather grand Marina de Cala d'Or simple and expensive yachts lie side by side at anchor. An international atmosphere prevails here with yachts from various countries. As one would expect of a good marina, it caters for the demands of the holiday sailors. It has specialist restaurants, good shopping, bars and flamenco shows, as well as tennis and riding clubs. A row of attractive apartments and villas continues along the cliff coast.

Porto Colóm (Pop. 400)

The extensive harbour basin is not deep enough for large vessels, so the local fishermen are not disturbed and can moor their boats in front of their cottages. This unspoilt friendly fishing village has been enlarged by a smart tourist development. In the unassuming local restaurants the fish is served fresh

Right: Magnificent harbour,
Porto Colóm

from the sea. Swimming facilities are not very good here. You can stroll to adjacent coves and the rocky beach at *Cala Marsal*.

  Instruction.

  Pedalos.

 Vall d'Or (9 holes).

 Celler Sa Sinia (Spanish).

 Post van (weekdays at noon).

 See Cala d'Or.

 Bus service via Felanitx–Manacor to Palma (several times daily).

Calas de Mallorca/Cala Domingo/Cala Murada

Calas de Mallorca

The holiday town of Calas de Mallorca developed on a remote, broad, rugged plateau of rock. It is within reach of fairly small sandy beaches that are quite charming. Hotels, apartment complexes and a holiday club present a monotonous façade of concrete. Below the town there is a small cove of sand and pebbles, *Cala Antena*. The sheer-faced cliff coastline with its deeply incised coves, many of which are practically inaccessible, creates a strange framework to this uniform holiday scene.

 Cala Antena, about 100 m long, sand and shingle with a beach bar, sun loungers and parasols.

 In numerous hotels; also children's pools.

 Club.   Pedalos.

 Also through hotels and tour companies.

 At the shopping centre.

 La Carreta (Spanish).

 In the hotels *Samoa* and *Los Chihuahuas*.

 Post van at 1 p.m. opposite the Hotel *Balmoral*.

 Dr Tortella, tel. 57 33 21; Dr Ingelmo y Garcia, tel. 57 34 35; Dr Saldañia, tel. 57 31 81.

 Bus service to Porto Cristo and Palma (several times daily).

Cala Domingo

From Calas de Mallorca it is a rather laborious 2-km walk to the very well kept resort of Cala Domingo. By car it is a round trip of about 10 km through the interior. This route is also served by a bus.

 The white sandy beach, framed by rocky cliffs, elegant villas and chalets, slopes gently to the sea, making it suitable for children. Sun loungers, parasols, bar and beach restaurant.

Cala Murada

This unspoilt modest development lies hidden away in pine woods. Small rocky inlets, seaweed and very little sand are the features of this small beach where there is only one kiosk and no facilities for water-sports.

 Hotel court at the only middle-range hotel, also public courts.

Sol y Vida (Majorcan/international cuisine); self-service shop.

Porto Cristo/Porto Cristo Novo/ Cala Estany

Porto Cristo

This lively fishing port in the middle of the east coast serves primarily as the principal departure point for the popular excursions in the area (Caves of *Drach* and *Hams*, drive-in safari park *Reserva Africana*, see page 88). Restaurants of varying categories, together with hotels which were built at the start of the tourist boom, await the visitors. Simple fish restaurants offer fresh seafood at reasonable prices.

At the fishing and yacht harbour there is a narrow, clean, white sandy beach.

In three hotels.

Porto Cristo Novo is the name of the new holiday area of the harbour township. It is proudly called the 'International Residential Centre'. German developers built bungalows here in a neo-Moorish style among small groups of palm trees. There is still plenty of land awaiting development. Two lovely, gently sloping sandy bays, well kept and sheltered from the wind, add a romantic touch to this prestigious project.

Cala Estany

About 8 km south of Porto Cristo is a remote sandy bay with a holiday village which still retains its charm. Fringing the bay are hotels, bungalows and villas built in neo-Moorish style on good-sized plots.

Extensive, sheltered, gently sloping beach of white sand. Sun loungers, parasols, small bar.

 Sailing instruction.

Bus Porto Cristo–Palma (several times daily).

S'Illot

A beautiful long sandy bay adorns the quiet rural development of S'Illot. It is particularly suited to families with young children. There is little in the way of organised entertainment. The favourite holiday pastime is walking on the beach and making trips along the varied coastline around Porto Cristo.

Both *Playa S'Illot* and *Cala Moreya* have extensive fine sandy beaches and are a real children's paradise. There are sun loungers and parasols.

In numerous hotels, some with children's pools.

 Pedalos.

Children love Majorca

Also through hotel reception and tour companies.

 Spanish, fish specialities.

 Medical centre, tel. 57 31 81.

Caves of *Drach* and *Hams*, *Reserva Africana* safari park. Bus service Porto Cristo–Palma (several times daily).

Cala Millor/Cala Bona (Costa de los Pinos)

Cala Millor

English and German café names await the holidaymaker on the fine white sandy beach of Cala Millor. The wide, open *Bahía de Artá* is quite spacious but there are masses of high-rise blocks. They are very functional and unimaginative and building still continues, but there is a cheerful beach promenade, green lawns and, in the background, groves of pine trees. The wide streets are packed with every sort of shop, restaurant and boutique. There are bodegas, bars and beer-cellars. For those who enjoy night life there is an extensive choice. And there is plenty to choose from for the dedicated sportsman.

Ideal for children, this 1½-km-long open, fine sandy beach slopes gradually to the sea. It is occasionally covered in small stones and seaweed. There are normal beach facilities.

In numerous hotels (heated in winter), some with children's pools.

 Also paragliding.

 Pedalos.

 Trips in glass-bottomed boats.

Tennis Centre (special courses). Floodlit sand courts; special courses in squash.

Relaxing at Porto Cristo

Two 9-hole courses at *Son Servera* and *Costa de los Pinos*.

6 lanes at *Los Toros* restaurant.

For long-stay winter visitors there are various entertainment and special interest programmes, as well as language courses in the club meetings organised by the major tour companies. Chess and card com-

Spectacular cliff-top scenery at Banyalbufar

La Baronia is the name of a former manor house (nowadays a pension) with a courtyard and 16th c. well. The road leads steeply down to the *Cala de Banyalbufar* where the old harbour in front of the cliffs and caves is the preserve of the local fishermen. Swimming is not recommended. The down-to-earth restaurant *Ca'n Bac* in the main street offers good Majorcan food.

Staying on the C-710 coast road and heading south, you come across the *Torre de las Ánimas*, built to warn off attacking Barbary pirates. In those days a chain of such towers surrounded the island. After 5 km you reach the friendly village of *Estellenchs* (150 m). There are wonderful walks on the northern foothills of the *Puig Galatzó* (1025 m). The old *Puerto de Estellenchs* is best reached on foot (1.5 km).

After a further 5 km you can enjoy the wide panorama from the *Mirador de R. Roca*. Souvenirs of every description are on sale next to the restaurant *Es Grau*. Steps lead to the impressive rock formations of the cliffs.

From the unassuming little country town of *Andraitx* (14 km) you come to the seaside resort of *San Telmo* (8 km), and after about 5 km to Puerto de Andraitx (see page 48).

After many twists and turns you go back via Paguera, Palma Nova (motorway from here), and past Cala Mayor to the metropolis of Palma (about 30 km).

The Northern Route

10 km

Palma

The northern route

Via the road to Sóller into the valley of the mountain torrent of La Calobra

Palma – Orient – Sóller – La Calobra – Torrente de Pareis (total distance about 175 km).

You could travel the 30 km from Palma to Sóller in leisurely fashion by taking the venerable old electric train. But there is so much to see along the C-711 road that going by car is an alternative not to be missed. Just 12 km north of the city it is well worth turning left off the main road. *Son Raxa*, a country manor house with gardens, lies about 1000 m from the road. The old mansion, which has an Italianate façade together with a pond, ornate pavilions and magnificent tropical plants, invites you to stop and relax. After about 4 km you reach the pleasant village of *Bunyola* with its surrounding olive plantations. From here the road branches towards *Orient*, climbing and zig-zagging.

Evergreen woods, wild countryside, ravines, splendid *fincas* (farmhouses), huge olive trees and sheep can all be seen along the 12-km detour to the mountain village of *Orient* (400 m). In this pleasant place there are two simple guest houses offering typical Majorcan meals. Roast sucking pig and rabbit are deliciously prepared here. The hotel *L'Ermitage* is in the style of a Majorcan country house and has an excellent menu featuring speciality dishes. Walking is the attraction of Orient, for example on the *L'Ofre* above

Bunyola spreads across the valley floor

Comasema. Even the easy route to the medieval *Castillo de Alaró* (800 m) leads to a wonderful panoramic view. The castle's defence towers have stood the test of time. On your way back to Bunyola another country house awaits: *La Alquería*, 4 km further on the left on the road to Sóller. Here too, the façade and gardens are worth seeing. Leaving the house, the road leads into the gentle rolling hills of *Las Gobias*. A signposted route takes two hours on foot to a scenic viewpoint with a panorama over the Bay of Palma.

A third country house is to be found after about 1000 m on the right-hand side of the road: *Son Alfabia*, on the western edge of the *Serreta de Alfabia*. This grand house was first the summer residence of the Moorish viziers and later, after the conquest of Majorca, the country house of the Catalonian King Jaime I. A splendid avenue of plane trees leads to the mansion which is surrounded by deciduous trees and luxuriant vegetation. In the entrance hall can be seen quotations from the Koran in Arabic script.

The road now climbs (3 km) via numerous switchbacks to the *Coll de*

Puig Mayor — Majorca's highest point

Sóller pass (496 m) which lies between the Sierra de Alfabia and the Teix. Palma, Bellver Castle and the coast of El Arenal can all be clearly seen. There are two rewarding routes along the summits for mountain walkers to choose between: you can climb to *Sierra de Alfabia* (1038 m; at 20.9 km marker) and scale the ridge away from the set path, or the second possibility is to tackle the *Teix* (1064 m). The route leads over the high plateau *Font de Sa Serp* with an easy ascent to the top. It is also possible to climb down to *Valldemosa*. Make sure you are properly equipped before attempting these climbs.

On the rest of the journey from Coll de Sóller down into the valley of Sóller you can show off your skilful cornering. The town and harbour come into view and

also the island's highest mountain, the *Puig Mayor* (1443 m).

Sóller (8 km) is a prosperous small town in the 'Valley of Oranges' (*Valle de los Naranjos*). These fruits as well as lemons, figs and almonds sell especially well in Belgium and France. Numerous tourists, particularly from these countries, spend their holidays here. This hospitable little town (Pop. 10,000) invites you to wander around its narrow little streets. The sights include the parish church of *San Bartolomé* (on the Plaza Maura), with a Baroque altar, and the *Estación F.C.* (railway station) a few yards away at the *Plaza España*. This is the terminus for the narrow-gauge railway from Palma and the tram stop for Puerto de Sóller (see page 49).

The harbour determined the town's history and importance. Phoenicians, Greeks and Romans used it as a trading base. The export of fruit to nearby countries still continues today.

A short pause at the *Plaza Maura*, the centre of this busy little town, makes a pleasant break. At one of the tables outside the cafés, bars and restaurants you can enjoy the lively atmosphere of this agreeable alternative to the metropolis of Palma. Almost all Majorca's imposing mountains tower around Sóller. For those waiting to assail the mountain peaks the route to take is via the settlement of *Alquería d'es Conte* to the mountain hamlet *Biniaraitx*. From here you can climb the *L'Ofre* (1091 m) The path snakes past the manor house of L'Ofre (500 m) up to the summit. On a clear day you have an outstanding view over the valley of Sóller and surrounding mountain ranges. From Sóller you can also drive through carefully tended orange groves (about 5 km) lying behind precision-built stone walls to the mountain hamlet of *Fornalutx* (180 m) (The rest of the journey is also possible from Biniaraitx.) This pretty village lying

Right: Torrente de Pareis — north coast

in the middle of orange groves with a beautiful old church square is also a good starting point for leisurely walks. Another 2 km further on you rejoin the C-710 road. The route meanders in wide bends past the viewing point *Ses Barques*, towards 'His Majesty' the *Puig Mayor*. The highest point on the island could in fact be conquered from *Son Torella* (900 m) without too much difficulty. However, owing to the presence of a military establishment, special permission — which may not be granted – is required to make this ascent.

Next you pass two reservoirs: the *Embalse de Cuber* and, in an exceptionally beautiful setting, the *Embalse de Gorg Blau*.

A Roman aqueduct marks the turning to La Calobra and to the gorge of the mountain torrent *Torrente de Pareis* (about 38 km from Sóller). Here you are presented with one of the most bizarre natural phenomena on Majorca. The drive through the valley, with its steep rock faces, and lined with olive trees and neatly built stone walls, over a well constructed pass is very impressive. The road to *La Calobra* leads through wild mountain scenery (reminiscent of the Dolomites) between the slopes of Puig Mayor and Puig Roig (1003 m). The resort is a popular place for tourists and day trippers, with its bars, a simple restaurant and similar accommodation. A rocky bay acts as a natural harbour and anchorage for the boat excursions from Puerto de Sóller. From here you can walk to the point where the Torrente de Pareis enters the sea. However, in summer the river bed is dried up.

To avoid the crowds you can return via *Cala Tuent* about 5 km away. It is a picturesque cove with a shingle beach and a few small boats. You can relax in this secluded spot and in the simple Majorcan restaurant.

You are past half way but not yet near the end of this circular tour. The C-710 takes you back to Sóller. From there after

about 12 km it leads to the colourful artists' village of *Deiá* (150 m). This small township is situated on a hill overlooking the sea. The modest parish church is built on the highest point and reached by narrow little streets. It is surrounded by olive groves and attractive estates and farmhouses in typical Majorcan style. The fortifications were the main base of the Cistercians, and in the Middle Ages the seat of the Visconti family. Nowadays artists and writers inhabit this village near the rugged, panoramic west coast. There are two four-star hotels and simple pensions for tourists. The nearest swimming is 30 minutes away at the fishing port of *Cala de Deiá*. There are many paths around and up to the Teix (1064 m) from Deiá.

The following drive to Valldemosa (10 km) has a lovely view of the coast. After negotiating a few bends you will see the 16th c. country house *Son Marroig* with a spectacular view of the peninsula *Na Foradada* and the rock formations of the *Costa Brava Mallorquina*. It is possible to visit the house and park.

About half-way you reach *Miramar*. The estate and about a dozen neighbouring farms used to belong to the Austrian Archduke Ludwig Salvator who had viewing platforms built along the coast in places. In the 13th c. the Majorcan philosopher and linguist Ramón Llull founded his famous school for oriental languages here (*Escola de Llengües Orientals*).

Finally we come to *Valldemosa* (400 m). The town and Carthusian monastery (*La Cartuja*), thanks to the well publicised relationship between the writer George Sand and the consumptive composer Frédéric Chopin, have done a lot for Majorca's history and tourism. Both these celebrities spent the winter of 1838/39 in two former cells of the monastery which were converted into comfortable private rooms. The souvenir trade still celebrates this event today in every feasible form, from the trashy to the

Valldemosa — house of Archduke Ludwig of Austria

artistic. This is despite the fact that the impulsive writer had very little positive to say about the land and its people in her early bestseller about the island, 'Un hiver à Majorque' (A Winter on Majorca). In August there is an annual Chopin Festival in Valldemosa with recitals by celebrated pianists from all over the world.

This small parish of 1200 inhabitants, surrounded by gently undulating hills and agricultural plantations, is one of the main attractions among the island's sights. Martin of Aragón established the Carthusian monastery in 1399. Its favourable climate and proximity to Palma made Valldemosa from early on the residence of the capital's prosperous new citizens. Moorish viziers and the Majorcan kings spent their summers here. The estates and manor houses in the surrounding area are indicative of the wealth of their former inhabitants. What were once the houses of the nobility in the village itself have become souvenir shops and restaurants.

The first glimpse of the monastery church from the small gardens near the car park is especially pretty. The church and cloisters are of 18th c. origin. It is worth visiting the powerful neo-Classical church building with frescos by the Carthusian Bayeu, and the retable 'La Piedad' by the Catalonian sculptor Adrián Ferrán. Among other items in the *sacristy* are vestments with valuable gold and silver embroidery and a Gothic reliquary. In the former *dispensary* at the cloisters there are 17th c. ceramics and glass containers, some still filled with old medicines. From the corridor you come to the old cells including the *prior's cell* (collection of documents, ceramics, paintings and a library of church history) and *Chopin's cell* with personal manuscripts and furnishings. There is also an old printing press à la Gutenberg, the Imprenta Guasp.

Also to be seen, near the parish church, is the house where Saint *Catalina Thomás* (16th c.) was born.

Hill walkers will find the climb over *Sa Coma* near the Teix (1064 m) interesting. It is possible to climb down to the pass at Sóller (Coll de Sóller).

The direct road to Palma gets narrower and after a few kilometres leads to the very narrow pass *S'Estret*. The subsequent stretch improves. Gnarled olive trees up to a thousand years old are gradually replaced by plantations of almond. After a total of 18 km you finally reach Palma.

Sun-soaked Selva with its mountain backdrop

The north-eastern route

Through vineyards to the monastery of the 'Brown Madonna'

Palma – Santa Maria – Alaró – Selva – Monasterio de Lluch – Inca – Binisalem – Palma (total distance about 100 km).

The C-713 heads north-east past the former airfield of Son Bonet. This is the old Roman road from Palma, which used to be known as *Palmaria*, to *Pollentia* on the coast (near the present-day town of Alcudia). After about 15 km you drive through *Santa Maria* (Pop. 3100) which was founded by the Moors. One of the island's wine-producing regions begins here. From the vines that are carefully protected by stone walls come the grapes from which the popular and delicious red wine is made. You can taste the wine for yourself either here or at nearby *Alaró* (9 km; turn left at Consell after 4 km). In the narrow little streets of this unspoilt country town (pop. 3300) you'll have difficulty in finding your way around – even before the wine-tasting! From here, partly by car, the remainder on foot, you can visit the *Castillo de Alaró* (medieval defence towers commanding superb views).

Through valleys surrounded by wooded hills, past vineyards and almond plantations, the route takes you via *Lloseta* with its cultivated fields to the busy village of *Selva* (pop. 300), a distance of 13 km altogether. Selva is dominated by its imposing *parish church* which is reached by a flight of steps lined by cypress trees.

After driving a further 12 km via *Caimari* along a well built stretch of road through mountains and mighty pine trees you arrive at the Monasterio de Lluch.

A few kilometres before the junction with the C-710 at the country house *Comafreda*, at a height of 500 m, climbers can find the way up to the *Puig de Massanella* (1348 m). The marked path is not too arduous and the view is worth the climb: Puig Mayor, Sierra and the sea in the west, the bays of Pollensa and Alcudia and in clear weather even the island of Minorca in the east.

The *Monasterio de Lluch* (400 m), impressively set in a vast, deep valley of cliffs and woods, is the most significant place for pilgrimages on Majorca. Here they worship *La Moreneta*, a madonna figure which dates from the 14th c., as originally did the monastery itself. In its present form the complex of buildings is about 300 years old. It has recently been renovated. As you approach, the woods and mountains recede to give you a clear view of this magnificent building. Through the manicured lawns of the *Clastre* (main square) you reach the monastery church which houses the 'Brown Madonna', *La Moreneta*. Today the monastery itself functions as a church boarding school. It does not have any marketable tourist attractions. In spite of crowds of sightseers this place manages to remain a haven of contemplation and meditation.

There are lovely walks and hikes starting from Lluch; the path from the mountain hamlet of Escora through Entreforc and the valley of Torrente de Pareis to the mouth of the torrent at *La Calobra* is particularly recommended. However, the river bed must be completely dry. It is a demanding walk but a marvellous experience. (La Calobra can also be reached by car from Lluch—about 21 km.)

We follow the picturesque mountain road back to Selva and continue 4 km to Inca.

Inca (Pop. 14,000), the third largest town in Majorca, is a centre of agriculture and of the leather, textile and shoe industries. Apart from the manufacturers' displays of goods to sell to the tourists, this bustling town has little to offer the visitor. A colourful weekly market takes place here every Thursday and the *Dijous Bo*, 'Good Thursday', a country folk-festival in November, still exists. Also noteworthy are the *parish church* with its enormous *clock tower* and the 18th c. monasteries of *San Francisco* and *Santo Domingo* with beautiful cloisters.

You must visit one of the *cellers*, the old wine cellars with their bulging barrels, where they also serve *porsella rostida* – roast sucking pig cooked in the traditional way of the region. It is worth waiting until you reach *Binisalem* (Pop. 4000) for the wine—it is the centre of production and renowned for its red wine. There is a whole range of cellars and bodegas here.

From Inca to Palma it is about another 28 km on the C-713.

North-eastern Route

10 km

The north coast

Two capes and two Roman towns.

Palma – Pollensa – Cabo Formentor – Alcudia – Cabo del Pinar – Palma (total distance about 200 km).

The C-713 leaves Palma in a north-easterly direction. After about 38 km, past the quaint little country church of *San Miguel* (13th c.), take a left turn to the *Cuevas de Campanet* (about 4 km). These limestone caves which are quite extraordinary in places were only discovered in 1945.

If you are travelling on a Sunday, then it is worth visiting the market at *La Puebla* (pop. 9000). Cross the main road C-713 and after 2 km you come to the little country town with its narrow streets. Its Sunday market is a popular meeting place.

Pollensa is about 20 km along the C-713. This small town (pop. 10,000) has retained its original character. Tiny narrow alleys wind through one of the oldest island communities, whose history goes back to the Romans. In the 18th c. parish church of *Nuestra Señora de los Angeles* can be seen a 'Virgin and Child' by the German painter Mosgraber. Other places to see include the *Iglesia de los Templarios*, a church built in the heyday of the Order of the Knights Templar (which was dissolved after the Crusades), the *Casa Consitorial* (town hall) and the former Dominican *Monastery of Santo Domingo*.

Short excursions could be made to the following places from here: *El Calvario* (Calvary on top of a hill) with its beautiful cypress-lined flight of steps; the hermitage of *Oratorio del Puig* (300 m) with superb views all round; or

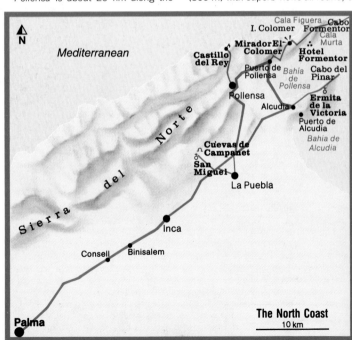

The North Coast
10 km

El Calvario

(about 6 km) the ruins of the *Castillo del Rey* (the King's Castle) on the coast, which once belonged to the Majorcan kings. From here you can enjoy a good view of the north coast.

Via Puerto Pollensa (see page 51) the round tour takes us to one of the most spectacular coastal regions of the island, the memorable *Cabo Formentor*. The well made mountain road was dynamited through the limestone cliffs.

The view stretches far back across the harbour at Pollensa. On the heights of *Mal Pas* (360 m) the first viewpoint, *Mirador El Colomer* (about 10 km), is to be found opposite the rocky island of the same name. From this marvellous vantage point, which is accessible from steps boldly cut into the rocks, you can take in the imposing panorama of the bizarre, craggy north coastline. You soon reach the highest point of the pass.

Splendid coastal scenery alternates with dense pine woods.

About 3 km further on stands the island's best-known luxury hotel, the *Hotel Formentor*, surrounded by pine woods and olive groves. This refuge for famous people on the picturesque golden sandy cove *Cala Pi* (see page 56) appears quite insignificant from the outside but is luxurious inside. Perhaps you will have an aperitif at the bar before taking a leisurely stroll in the grounds.

The pass road winds between steep walls of limestone cliffs and sheer drops, surrounded by breathtaking views, past the small beach of *Cala Murta*, through the tunnel of *Es Fumat* (334 m; access to

viewing point very difficult) and for another 13 km down to the lighthouse *Faro de Formentor* (209 m). This is the most northerly point of Majorca. This exciting but tiring drive is rewarded with the view, in good visibility, of the bay of Pollensa and perhaps even the eastern tip of Minorca.

Follow the same route back to Puerto Pollensa from where it is about another 10 km to the medieval fortified town of *Alcudia* (Pop. 3500), at the other end of the Bay of Pollensa. This town was also founded by the Romans. The fortifications from the time of Jaime II's regency are impressive and unmistakable landmarks of the former town. Two well

Faro de Formentor lighthouse

preserved town gates are reminders of the splendour and misery brought by changing fortunes; the Roman island metropolis Pollentia was burned down by the Vandals about 400 A.D., rebuilt by the Moors as Alcudia and elevated to a military town by Jaime II. Even the parish church of *San Jaime* (16th c.) used to be a corner bastion of the town walls. The reliefs around the Gothic high altar are depicted in strong colours. On the southern edge of the town on the road to Puerto de Alcudia (see page 53) is the *Teatro Romano*, a Roman amphitheatre. On the same road you turn off towards *Bon Aire*, an attractively situated resi-dential development with a vast yacht harbour.

For about 11 km the drive continues over another impressive mountain road along a bizarre cliff coast, with more wonderful views of the *Formentor* peninsula, to the *Cabo del Pinar*: pine woods, unspoilt rocky coves and picturesque places to bathe, without too much bustle during the week. The final third of the route is the ascent to the primitive little *Ermita de la Victoria* church with lovely views. The mountain road ends before you get to the cape at a restricted military zone. Take the same route back to Alcudia and then the C-713 for about 53 km to Palma.

Alcudia — Roman theatre

The eastern route

From the monastery on the hill to the interior

Palma – Algaida – Mt. Randa – Manacor – Petra – Sineu – Sencelles – Palma (total distance about 145 km).

The C-715 is a well built road that is heavily used. It heads east and the pleasant little country town of *Algaida* (pop. 3500) is at the end of a straight stretch (about 30 km).

Directly on the main thoroughfare is the rustic restaurant *Ca'l Dimoni* which serves lamb and pork chops and the popular stew *sopas mallorquinas* (see recipe page 15). Head south through the town towards Lluchmayor for about 3 km, then take a left turn and after a rough stretch of some 2 km you come to the hamlet of *Castellitx*. Here can be seen what is said to be the oldest Christian chapel in Majorca, the *Ermita de la Pau* (A.D.1236), with a beautiful doorway.

Back on the main road after about 2 km you pass the town and the mountain both called *Randa* (280 m). This uphill winding stretch through bush and pine woods leads, in about a kilometre, to the monastery and church of *Nuestra Señora de Gracia*, perched on the steep hillside. In another kilometre you reach the *Santuario San Honorato*, with a simple chapel; from here there are good views over the Bay of Palma. After a further 1½ km you

come to the *Santuario de Nuestra Señora de Cura*, one of the historic places of pilgrimage on the island. It was here that the poet and philosopher Ramón Llull wrote his celebrated work 'Ars Magna'. There is an uninterrupted panorama over the countryside and sea around Palma.

From *Randa* you rejoin the C-715 after some 8 km at *Montuiri* (pop. 5000) which extends picturesquely over a hill. The town is famous for its sausages.

On the route east, after a further 10 km, you drive through the long main street of the village of *Villafranca* (pop. 2200). Wine and agriculture are the basis of the economy here and the roadside kiosks sell the juiciest garlic on the island!

9 km further on lies the second largest town on the island, *Manacor* (Pop. 19,000). The economy of this regional centre is based on agriculture, furniture and the production of artificial pearls. The pointed tower of the parish church of *Dolores de Nuestra Señora* (partly 15th c.), visible from a long way away, dominates the busy town like an admonishing finger. The former monastery of *Santo Domingo* (17th/18th c.) with its beautiful chapel, and the *Torre de Ses Puntes*, remains of the old 15th c. town fortifications, are worth a visit. In the main street you cannot fail to notice the popular Majorcan artificial pearls displayed for sale to the tourists.

Returning along the C-715 you come to the turning for *Petra* (Pop. 4500). This delightful little market town (about 8km) presents a picture of tasteful unity. There are two churches in this lively community, whose most famous son was Fray Junipero Serra. In 1713 he was born here as José Miguel, and he went on in his capacity as a missionary to found the Californian towns of Los Angeles, San Francisco, San Diego, San José and Monterey. There is a monument to him in this little town and a bust in the Capitol in Washington. The well preserved house where he was born is in simple Majorcan style and serves as his memorial. The parish church of *San Pedro* with a Gothic altar (16th/18th c.) and the monastery church of *San Bernadino* can be seen on the way round the town. About 4 km south-west on a hill of 300 m stands the *Ermita de Bonany* (17th c.) where the (allegedly) thousand-year-old image of the Madonna *Mare de Deú de Bonany* is revered. It is to be found on the high altar. There is a wonderful view from the hermitage.

From *Petra* you travel some 10 km further towards *Sineu* (Pop. 6000) along a road lined with cultivated fields surrounded by stone walls, hilly land, pines and olive trees. Sineu is a charming little town with narrow streets. Geographically it lies in the centre of Majorca. On Wednesdays it has a lively market.

About 5 km further towards Inca the straight road is edged with almond trees and runs through a wooded landscape. The road branches off to the left towards Costitx (2 km) into scenic hilly countryside. It is the small personal discoveries which make this short detour on good minor roads a rewarding experience. In the little parish church of the old-fashioned village of *Costitx* there is a 14th c. image of the Madonna that was supposed to have been found by children in an apple tree. *Sencelles* (about 14 km) is popular with artists. There is a valuable marble altar in the parish church of *San Pedro*. The village (pop. 2000; 118 m) has magnificent views of the surrounding chain of mountains.

Passing through the dilapidated hamlet of *Biniali*, 12 km further on through *Santa Maria* you reach the C-713. From here it is about another 14 km to Palma.

The south-eastern route

To the stalactitic caves of the east coast

Palma – Lluchmayor – Felanitx (Castillo de Santueri) – Porto Cristo – Cuevas del Drach and dels Hams – Cuevas de Artá – Capdepera – Artá – Palma (total distance about 185 km).

The section of motorway in the direction of Santanyi as far as Ca'n Pastilla speeds up the drive from Palma along the C-717 towards the south-east of the island. You can recognise the windmills of *Sant Jordi* in the distance. *Lluchmayor* (pop. 12,000) can be reached either on the C-717 or from Playa de Palma via El Arenal, about 24 km either way. This simple little town has a place in the island's history. Just north of the town about half-way to Mount Randa the battle between King Pedro IV of Aragón and King Jaime III was fought in 1349; this was to lead to the end of the Kingdom of Majorca (see page 7).

After some 13 km the relatively straight road comes to busy *Campos del Puerto* (pop. 6500). From here you drive in a north-easterly direction through changing scenery to *Felanitx* (pop. 12,000). It lies in front of the *Puig San Salvador* (500 m), a place of pilgrimage (about 6 km) with a lovely view.

This picturesque old town with the splendid 18th c. parish church of *San Miguel* is renowned for its white wine, but its main economy is centred on majolica and glass manufacture.

6 km south-east of *Felanitx* stands the *Castillo de Santueri*. A former medieval castle, it is one of Majorca's oldest defences with its pinnacled towers. Its function was to protect *Porto Colóm*, the old harbour of Felanitx.

About 10 km north of *Porto Colóm* you reach the coast road C-717 with its cluster of beaches and resorts (see page 58) and follow it to the *Cuevas del Drach* on the southern edge of *Porto Cristo*. The 'Dragon Caves' used to be underground refuges in the Middle Ages. They were discovered at the end of the 19th c. by a Frenchman, E.A. Martel. The underground lake, some 177 m long, on average 40 m wide and up to 9 m deep, is named after its discoverer. The limestone caves extend over nearly 2 km and are amongst the largest in Europe. A boat trip across the clear lake under the fairy-tale sky of the stalactites is to be recommended. About 3 km west of Porto Cristo the *Cuevas dels Hams* lie hidden. They were discovered in 1906. *Hams* is Majorcan for harpoon and describes the shape of the stalactites in the 350-m-long caves. The glistening

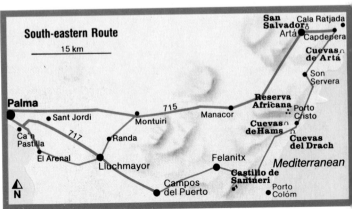

The parish church of San Miguel at Felanitx

stalactites and stalagmites project like giant arrows. The underground lake, called *Mar de Venecia* (Sea of Venice) is crystal-clear with a mirror-like surface.

Continuing along the north-east coast you can, after 5 km, take a detour to the *Reserva Africana*, a safari park of 40 ha. with species ranging from antelopes, elephants, rhinos and hippos to waterbucks and zebras as well as numerous birds.

Continuing for about 20 km along the coast via *Son Servera*, past well known resorts, you arrive at *Capdepera* (pop. 3000) which is charming and well kept. A visit to the Moorish castle is well worth while. Steps lead up from the *Plaza España* but it is also possible to make the rather perilous drive up past the *Plaza José Antonio* and the town hall. Once you get to the ruin you have a marvellous view over the town and picturesque countryside. Afterwards you can unwind at the harbour of *Cala Ratjada* (see page 68) or begin the return journey on the C-715 (10 km) to *Artá* (pop. 5800). The small medieval country town in a charming hillside setting has as its main attraction the 19th c. pilgrims' church of *San Salvador*, which was built on a little hill on top of the remains of the town wall and consequently has good views. It is connected by a flight of steps, flanked by cypress trees, to the Gothic parish church of the *Transfiguración del Señor* (13th/16th c.) which stands below it. On the *Calvario* steps are representations of the 'Way of the Cross'. The whole site offers marvellous views over the houses of the nobility of this town, which blossomed under Jaime I. The *Museo Local de Artá* contains many exhibits from prehistoric times.

The C-715 takes you the 80 km back to Palma.

The 'Way of the Cross'

The island of Cabrera

Cabrera, 'Island of the Blue Grotto'

If a short sea journey to an almost uninhabited island appeals to you then you can sail from Palma (twice weekly) to the island of *Cabrera*. You need to plan your day, take sufficient provisions with you and hope that Neptune does not get angry before the evening. Should the return journey have to be cancelled because of heavy seas then this rugged island will have to become an open-air hotel! It has neither restaurant nor any kind of accommodation. The journey by sea (about 50 km) takes approximately 2½ hours.

The archipelago consists of other smaller islands, the largest being the *Isla Conejera* (Rabbit Island). As you go into the imposing sheltered natural harbour through its 300-m-wide entrance you will be greeted by a solid 14th c. defence tower which was unable to defend the island against Barbary pirates. It makes a good viewpoint. A small monument at the harbour commemorates 8000 Frenchmen who were banished here as prisoners of war from 1809 to 1814 after the Battle of Bailén against Napoleon.

Nowadays the lighthousekeepers and their families are the only inhabitants of Cabrera. Wild goats graze on the sparse vegetation of this arid limestone island. The highest point is the 172-m *Puig de la Guardia*. Away from the 5-sq.-km bay of the harbour there is not much to see. In good weather there is a fascinating boat trip (30 minutes) to *Cueva Azul*. The Blue Grotto is so called because of the deep blue colour of the incoming light which is caused by the reflections of the white sandy sea-bed below the inflowing water.

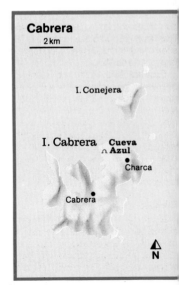

Cabrera
2 km

I. Conejera

I. Cabrera   Cueva
∩ **Azul**
●
Charca

●
Cabrera

▲
N

Useful things to know...

Before you go
Insurance
Spain now has a reciprocal agreement with Great Britain under which free medical treatment can be obtained for those entitled to it at home. To get this benefit it is essential to be in possession of form E.111 obtainable from the DHSS (application forms from the DHSS or at main post offices). This agreement does not provide full cover and you are strongly recommended to take out holiday insurance with a reputable company. Most tour operators include this as part of their package.

What to take
Most items that you would normally need on holiday can be obtained on the island. Good sun-glasses are indispensable and can be bought locally, but if you need special glasses or a particular suntan lotion, etc., it is advisable to take these with you. Photographers who use top-quality film should buy this at home; don't forget a lens-hood and filters.

First-aid kit. There are plenty of chemists *(farmacias)* in the towns and tourist centres. However, prescribed medicines and any particular medicaments that you normally use at home should be taken with you, together with remedies for stomach upsets, headaches, etc. An elastic bandage, plasters and antiseptic cream are useful for minor injuries.

Climate
The evenly temperate Mediterranean climate of Majorca ensures the visitor a pleasant holiday at every season. In summer the average temperature is 25° and in winter 10°. The relative humidity is only 70%. Rainfall is greatest during the winter months, the summer being sunny and dry but not unpleasantly hot.

Getting to Majorca
By air: Most visitors to Majorca travel by air. There are direct flights from London to Son San Juan Airport from where taxis and coaches convey passengers to Palma (about 15 minutes). There is a wide choice of package holidays using charter flights, many of which operate all the year round.

By sea: There are car ferries to Palma from the Spanish mainland ports of Barcelona (8 hours), Valencia (9 hours) and Alicante (11 hours).

Immigration and Customs Regulations
For entry to Spain and the Balearic Islands a British Visitor's Passport is sufficient for a stay of up to three months.

Customs: Duty-free allowances for EEC countries are as follows: 300 cigarettes or 75 cigars or 400 gr. tobacco; 1.5 litres of spirits (over 22% vol) or 3 litres of sparkling or fortified wine and 5 litres of other wine; 90 cc. perfume and 0.375 litres of toilet water. If any of the above have been bought in a duty-free shop or on a ship or aircraft the allowances are approximately one third less.

During your stay
Currency
The Spanish unit of currency is the peseta (abbreviated to ptas. in the plural). 1 pta. = 100 céntimos; 5 ptas. = 1 duro. There are coins in denominations of 1, 2, 5, 10, 25, 50, 100 and 500 ptas. and banknotes for 100, 200, 500, 1000, 2000, 5000 and 10,000

ptas. The exchange rate fluctuates and it is worth comparing the rates offered by various banks and exchange offices. You are advised to take most of your money in the form of travellers' cheques or Eurocheques and not to carry large sums of money about with you.

Eurocheques can be cashed on production of a cheque card and passport. You can also change money at exchange kiosks and at many hotels, but the rate is not as favourable as the official bank rate.

Drinking water

The tap water is suitable for brushing your teeth but not for drinking. Bottled water is cheap and easily available.

Electricity

Mainly 220 volts, but occasionally you may find 100–125 volts. You will need a Continental adaptor.

Opening times

Banks: Open every day except Sunday everywhere on the island from 9 a.m. until 1 or 2 p.m.

Post offices: Monday to Friday from 9 a.m. until 2 p.m. The main post office is also open from 4 to 7 p.m.

Shops: They are generally open from 9 a.m. until 1.30 p.m. and from 4 or 5 p.m. until 7 p.m., but in summer they often stay open later in the evenings. Most shops are closed on Saturday afternoon and Sunday.

Post

A letter from Majorca to Great Britain normally takes four to six days. Stamps are available from tobacconists (*tabacalera* or *estanco*) and your hotel reception as well as from post offices.

Religious services

Roman Catholic services held in Majorca's churches are conducted in Spanish, but in the resorts and tourist areas many denominations hold services in English.

Street and place names

Street and place names (on maps and road signs) are increasingly written in the Majorcan dialect. This means that they are often different from the accepted Spanish name.

Telephone

International telephone calls can be dialled direct from public telephone boxes in all main resorts. You will need a plentiful supply of 25, 50 and 100 peseta coins (5 peseta coins are only of use for local calls). The international dialling code to the United Kingdom is 07 44.

Tipping

When giving a tip (*la propina*) you should be fair but not extravagant. Waiters usually expect between 5% and 10% of the bill. In the hotel it is advisable to tip at the end of each week instead of waiting until the end of your holiday. Should the service and courtesy leave a lot to be desired then show your dissatisfaction in the amount of the tip.

Traffic regulations

The speed limit for cars in towns is 60 km p.h., on main roads 100 km p.h. and on motorways 120 km p.h. You must sound your horn on approaching a bend during the day but the use of the horn is prohibited in towns between 11 p.m. and 6 a.m. At night watch out for vehicles using only side lights. It is compulsory to wear seat belts on main roads.

On Majorca the road network is

generally of a good standard. The best advice is 'drive carefully' — and remember to drive on the right.

Transport in Majorca

Buses: There are bus connections from Palma to Cala d'Or, Cala Ratjada, Playa de Palma/El Arenal, Esporlas, Banyalbufar, Estellenchs, Felanitx, Galilea, Porto Cristo, Puerto de Alcudia, Andraitx, Puerto Pollensa, Santanyi/Cala Figuera and Playa de Poniente (via Portals Nous, Palma Nova, Magaluf, Santa Ponsa, Paguera, Camp de Mar and Puerto de Andraitx), as well as Valldemosa, Deiá and Puerto de Sóller.

Car hire: Cars can be hired through international and local companies and in the smaller resorts through your hotel reception or tour company. A valid driving licence is required and you must be over 21 years of age. Lead-free petrol is available at Son San Juan airport and at selected filling stations.

Railways: The rail 'network' of Majorca consists of two routes, one from Palma to Inca and the other from Palma to Sóller. From Sóller an 'old-timer' tram continues to Puerto de Sóller. All railway buffs will enjoy the trip on this line.

Taxis: For journeys in Palma itself the fare is displayed on the meter. There is a price list (*la tarifa*) for the chief long-distance routes which every driver has and must show on request.

Inter-island transport: There are **ferry services** between Palma and Ibiza, Minorca (Ciudadela) and Cabrera; also from Alcudia to Minorca (Ciudadela), and from Ibiza to Formentera.

Air services operate daily between the islands of Majorca, Ibiza and Minorca.

Important addresses
Consulates
British Consulate
Plaza Mayor 3D,
Palma; tel. (971) 71 20 85, 71 24 45.

Tourist Offices
In Great Britain:
Spanish National Tourist Office
57 St James's Street,
London SW1A 1LD;
tel. (01) 499 0901.

In Majorca:
Oficina de Información Turistica
Avda. Jaime III 10;
tel. (971) 21 22 16.

Emergency: tel. 22 21 79.

Traffic Police
Palma, Plaza General García Ruiz;
tel. 22 54 40.

Clinics and Hospitals:
Son Dureta, Social Security Hospital,
Palma;
tel. 28 91 00.

Leisurely sightseeing in Palma

Useful words and phrases

Although English is widely understood in those parts of Spain which are frequented by tourists, the visitor will undoubtedly find a few words and phrases of Spanish very useful. In general pronunciation is not too difficult; ñ sounds very like the *ni* in *onion*; *x*, and *c* before *e* and *i*, are usually lisped; a final *d* generally becomes *th* (as in *thin*) and a medial *d* like *th* in *the*. *ll* should be pronounced as if it were *ly* - or in some places *y*.

A word ending in a vowel or in *n* or *s* is normally stressed on the last syllable but one; a word ending in any other consonant on the final syllable. Any exceptions bear an accent on the stressed syllable.

please	¡por favor!	chemist	farmacia
thank you (very much)	¡(muchas) gracias!	toilet	retrete
yes/no	si/no	ladies	señoras
excuse me	¡con permiso!	gentlemen	señores
do you speak English?	¿Habla Usted inglés?	engaged	ocupado
I do not understand	No entiendo	free	libre
good morning	¡Buenos días!	entrance	entrada
good afternoon	¡Buenas tardes!	exit	salida
good night	¡Buenas noches!	today/tomorrow	hoy/mañana
goodbye	¡Adiós!	Sunday/Monday	domingo/lunes
how much?	¿Qué precio tiene?	Tuesday/Wednesday	martes/miércoles
I should like	Quisiera	Thursday/Friday	jueves/viernes
a room with private bath	un habitación con baño	Saturday/holiday	sábado/día festivo
the bill, please!	¡la cuenta (la nota) por favor!		
everything included	todo incluido		
when is it open?	¿A qué hora está abierto?		
when is it shut?	¿A qué hora se cierra?		
where is . . . street?	¿Dónde está la Calle . . .?		

the road to . . .	el camino para . . .?	0	cero
how far?	¿Qué distancia?	1	un(o)
to the left/right	a la izquierda/direcha	2	dos
straight on	siempre derecho	3	tres
post office	correo	4	cuatro
railway station	estación	5	cinco
Town Hall	Ayuntamiento	6	seis
exchange office	Cambio	7	siete
police station	commisaría	8	ocho
public telephone	teléfono público	9	nueve
Tourist Information Office	Oficina de Información de Turismo	10	diez
doctor	médico	11	once
		12	doce
		20	veinte
		50	cincuenta
		100	ciento

Index

Original German text: Robert P. Hertwig. English translation: Julie Waller. Cartography: Gert Oberländer. Illustrations: Spanish National Tourist Office; Travel Trade Photography (pages 10, 18, 40, 43); Chris Williams (pages 3, 4, 9, 17, 20, 22, 25, 29, 30, 32, 42, 44, 45, 56, 69, 70, 74); P. Waring (pages 35, 39, 54, 84).
Series Editor — English edition: Alec Court.

© Verlag Robert Pfützner GmbH, München
    Original German edition

© Jarrold Publishing, Norwich, Great Britain 1/90
    English language edition worldwide

The publishers have made every endeavour to ensure the accuracy of this publication but can accept no responsibility for any errors or omissions. They would, however, appreciate notification of any inaccuracies to correct future editions.

Printed in Italy

ISBN 0-7117-0470-8